MIND

Peter Nobes had his first experience of the Alexander Technique in 1988 and qualified as an Alexander teacher in 1993. He is based in central London and has taught Alexander in ten countries on three continents. He has been training *Mindfulness in 3D* Alexander teachers since 2013. Peter is a member of Alexander Technique International. When he isn't teaching Alexander, he builds wooden boats, plays Bach on his recorder and dances Argentine Tango.

Mindfulness in 3D

The Alexander Technique for the 21st century

Peter Nobes

Illustrations by Hannah Snaith

THE REAL PRESS
www.therealpress.co.uk

Published in 2018 by the Real Press.
www.therealpress.co.uk
© Peter Nobes Illustrations are © Peter Nobes and
Hannah Snaith

ISBN (print) 9781912119578
ISBN (ebooks) 9781912119592

For Jai and Cherry, and Lata

Acknowledgements

I've crossed paths with many inspiring Alexander people over the years; I owe them so much. Eileen Stratton, David Gorman, Margaret Edis, Ann Penistan, Barry Kantor, Penny O'Connor, Antoinette Kranenburg, Galit Zeif, Gilles Estran, Fiona Cranwell, Cécile Rist, Kajsa Ingemansson – the list could be so much longer!

Thank you to Eve Salomon, Marianne Promberger, Michael Ashcroft and Jean Marray for reading the manuscript and making helpful suggestions. Special thanks to my publisher, David Boyle; my editor, Andy Jacques; and my illustrator, Hannah Snaith.

Contents

Introduction – 5

1/Everything is effortless – 9
2/A short chapter on posture – 16
3/The effortful life – 18
4/The frustrating search for solutions – 26
5/You don't look the way you think you do – 35
6/A mode for everything we do – 41
7/Ageing is a choice – 52
8/ Rediscovering your 'UP', finding your balance – 60
9/Freedom to choose – 75
10/Embracing change – 108

Appendix/F. M. Alexander – 127

More resources – 129

Introduction

"My work is an exercise in finding out what thinking is."
Frederick Matthias Alexander

There's an awkward moment at social occasions when I am asked what I do for a living and I say I teach the Alexander Technique. I usually get one of two replies: "What's that?" or "Oh, good posture!"

The Alexander Technique isn't about posture. But, on the other hand, I can't easily sum up in one sentence what it *is* about, despite having made my living teaching it for quarter of a century. The art of living in the here-and-now? Mindfulness in action? The secret of Zen for our time? It certainly has more in common with Zen, Stoicism and Existentialism than it does with 'bodywork', or things like yoga and Pilates that everyone tends to associate it with.

You can understand why people get the wrong idea. Many of the popular books on the Alexander Technique are easy to read, whereas Alexander's own books are difficult. Why the difference? It's because they aren't describing the same thing. The popular books are mostly talking about bodies and posture, whereas Alexander was struggling to put into words something that he felt could be humanity's next evolutionary step. It is clear from his writings that he didn't really understand how evolution works, but nonetheless he knew he had discovered something ground-breaking and enormously life-changing.

The word 'posture' doesn't occur once in Alexander's most accessible book, *Use of the Self*, and the chapter titles include 'The Golfer Who Cannot Keep His Eyes on the Ball' and 'The Stutterer'. Chapters in one of his earlier books, *Constructive Conscious Control of the Individual*, include 'Unduly Excited Fear Reflexes, Uncontrolled Emotions, and Fixed Prejudices', 'Psycho-Physical Equilibrium', ''Knowing Oneself'', 'Memory and Feeling', 'Complexity and Complications in Relation to Stress and Strain' and 'Sensory Appreciation in its Relation to Happiness'. He clearly wasn't talking about bodies!

Over the past two and a half decades, I have helped people change their lives in all sorts of ways using the Alexander Technique, including 'knowing themselves', letting go of fixed prejudices, and, perhaps most importantly, achieving happiness. Yes, most of them have improved their posture as well, but that was a side benefit.

The Alexander Technique has changed my life too. It helped me go from being too shy to look people in the eye when I started learning it in my early thirties to being enormously confident. I went from shaking with fear if I had to do a presentation to twenty people – even if I knew them well – to becoming a performer, enjoying getting on stage and presenting talent shows at international conferences.

That isn't about posture. It isn't even about my

body. But then the Alexander Technique isn't about bodies. And most of our aches, pains and problems aren't about our bodies either. As you are about to find out, they are about the way we do things. This book will, I hope, get you thinking about how you do things.

Becoming aware of how you do things and making new choices only works when you are conscious; when you are mindful. You can't change when you are on 'autopilot' – change involves switching off autopilot and being more mindful. But the Alexander Technique is not about being more mindful of your body, or 'getting back in touch with your body', because you ARE your body. It's about mind/body unity, about being your authentic self, living in the here-and-now.

With the Alexander Technique, you'll find it's possible to do almost anything – mind and body – without strain or effort, and do it better. You'll feel a sense of ease, freedom and aliveness you probably haven't experienced since childhood – and look good too, and be happier. And find your new bodily freedom and more conscious mind is like life in three dimensions.

1
Everything is effortless

"The Alexander Technique eludes precise definition because it involves a new experience – the experience of gradually freeing oneself from the domination of fixed habits."

Michael Gelb, Alexander Teacher, author and renowned speaker on creativity and innovation

Everything is effortless. Standing is effortless. Running is effortless. Walking up stairs is effortless. Sitting upright at your desk is effortless. Right? It's all so effortless you don't even know you've got a body. Thinking is effortless too, and decision-making. And you've chosen the life you're living, and you like your size and shape and the way you look. You're happy.

If that isn't how you live, and you would like it to be, maybe you should learn the Alexander Technique.

I ask all my new clients why they want to learn the Alexander Technique and none of them ever say "for happiness". Or "to be effortless" or "to have more choices" or "to be more mindful". Now and then, someone says they would like to learn it so they look better, and very occasionally they give me an intriguing reason, like "I want to stop feeling nervous when I meet new people."

One person told me: "I want to learn it because I heard it's like Cognitive Behavioural Therapy." I was impressed, because the Alexander Technique does have parallels with CBT. But he went on to say "But I looked it up online and it seems it's about posture."

Most people who come to me say it's because they have neck- or back-pain, and they think it's caused by bad posture. And, interestingly, they usually come to me when they have exhausted all the other options: they've been to their GP, the physio and then the osteopath. They've tried yoga and Pilatcs.

Does the Alexander Technique help them? Yes. One of my clients had back pain so bad she couldn't sit and had to use a standing-desk at work. She came to me after trying everything else. Within four sessions she was sitting comfortably.

After a long study of its effectiveness, the *British Medical Journal* concluded that the Alexander Technique, coupled with exercise, "seems the most effective and cost-effective option for the treatment of back pain in primary care."

We don't actually 'treat' back pain, but people could still save themselves effort, time and money by coming for Alexander first. [1]

---

[1] Randomised controlled trial of Alexander technique lessons, exercise, and massage (ATEAM) for chronic and recurrent back pain: *BMJ* 2008;337:a2656.

We can explore this issue about posture by looking at an example of modern humanity you're probably all aware of – the Phone Zombie. There are two things that fascinate me about these people: the contortions they pull their bodies into, and the mindless ways in which they stop dead in the middle of the pavement to read a text, blocking the way for everyone else, or walk out of shops with their eyes on the phone and bump into each other.

Someone stopped suddenly in front of me on the steps at my local Underground station curved tightly over his phone with such desperation and pain in his face, I thought he must have had a message saying someone had died. As I squeezed past him I saw he was taking his next turn in Scrabble.

Let's examine the Phone Zombie's posture before we talk about his mindlessness: knees and hips locked, exaggerated lumbar curve, neck severely bent. No wonder people are in pain! I only have to

stand like this for 30 seconds and those areas start hurting, and I can't bend my neck to 90 degrees the way I see some people do. If we were to teach the Phone Zombie 'good posture' we might get him to align his 'key points: his ear, shoulder, hip joint, knee and ankle all in a vertical line. But doing so would entail stiffness, pulling and tension. And to keep his phone eight inches from his eyes he's going to have to hold his arm up, with all the effort that involves. Surely life should be simpler than this?

Recently, I watched two girls sitting in a restaurant: a fourteen-year-old and her six-year-old sister. The six-year-old was lightly upright, easy, effortless and bouncy, but her sister was heavily slumped. If her back wasn't hurting yet, it soon would be. If her parents took her to a physiotherapist she'd be shown 'good posture', 'core strength' and how to sit properly. She'd be taught which muscles to strengthen so she could hold herself upright, and to align those key points.

She would probably learn to do it, but sitting like that takes so much effort she'd almost certainly let herself slump again when no-one was looking. Wouldn't it be simpler if she could just get back the light, bouncy thing her sister still has?

She can. Why can't the Phone Zombie learn to have the effortlessly upright body that the six-year-old has? He can, with the Alexander Technique.

There's something else: natural movement. This doesn't just apply to how we sit or use our phones. I live less than a mile from the start of the London Marathon and, every year, I watch 40,000 people stream past the end of my road in a block that lasts over an hour. It's inspiring but it's also very revealing: 40,000 people, and all the different styles of running.

Some of them move lightly and effortlessly, others move heavily and effortfully. Some of them are frowning, looking down at the ground, running only to get to the end or to get a 'personal best', and others look as if they're enjoying it and are aware of their surroundings. *The Art of Running with the Alexander Technique* says: "It is possible to move in many different ways... sometimes the variations can be pretty funny..."[2]

This diversity is so common we might be tempted to think it's perfectly natural. But is it? I wonder what it would be like watching 40,000 deer run past. Or cheetahs? Or giraffes? They'd have just one way of moving.

Late in her life, my mother lost most of her sight. She wasn't able to recognise her friends by their faces or their shape, or by the way they dressed, but she had just enough vision to be able to tell them apart by the way they moved.

You can't tell cats apart by how they move. You can't tell elephants apart by how they move. Or those deer. Or snow geese or grizzly bears. They just move like cats, like elephants, like deer. It's only humans,

---

[2] *The Art of Running with the Alexander Technique.* Malcolm Balk and Andrew Shields. Ashgrove Publishing. 2000. p.97.

and especially adult humans, that you can tell apart by the way they move. Why? We've 'forgotten' how to do the natural thing, and have to use strategies to determine how to move.

Some of these strategies are unconscious, like the fourteen-year-old slumping in the restaurant. Or pulling ourselves into distorted curves because we need to get our eyes eight inches from our phones. Some are chosen, like walking with a swagger. Some are even found in coaching manuals.

I browsed a book on running and found eight pages of advice on 'how to run' – gait, posture, where to hold your arms, when to breathe. I bet the eleven Kenyans who won medals for athletics at the 2012 Olympic Games didn't have to read it, or the Kenyans who've won most of the London Marathons in recent years.

In his book *The Lost World of the Kalahari*, Laurens van der Post describes a group of Bushmen running all day after a herd of eland, while he followed them in his Land Rover.[3] He said: "I am certain they ran as only the Greek who brought the news of Marathon to Athens could have run."

Who taught them to run like that? It seems that there's a natural way of running that we shouldn't need to be taught.

After all, we all knew how to run when we were younger. If you want to see good, natural running in the UK, watch girls before they reach their teens,

---

[3] Chatto and Windus, 1988 p.200.

before they have become aware of their bodies. Watch boys before they start to run in a way that they think looks, or feels, 'cool' or 'tough'. That six-year-old in the restaurant probably runs in a light, natural way. And her sister almost certainly doesn't.

Can't we get it back? We can – with the Alexander Technique. As one of my clients said in an email to me: "I have to tell you about my Alexander running... the only way I can describe it is that I ran like a Kenyan!"

There's one natural way to move and there are a thousand unnatural, unattractive and inefficient ways. What is the natural thing? It's attractive and efficient. No 'core strength', no 'shoulders back', just graceful movement and bright eyes, and a body so easy you won't know it's there.

The Phone Zombie can learn to liberate himself; to stay effortlessly upright and to float his phone up to where he can see it. And to stay mindful of his surroundings as he does it.

2
A short chapter on posture

"You think my work is a physical thing; I tell you it is perhaps the most mental thing that has ever been discovered."
F. M. Alexander

The Alexander Technique will give you better posture, but so will yoga and Pilates. Your physiotherapist or your osteopath can give you advice on improving your posture, and so can your mum: "Stand up straight! Pull your shoulders back!"

But why do people care so much about their posture? The photos in *The Lost World of the Kalahari* clearly show that the Bushmen don't need to be concerned about their posture. Refugees fleeing from bombed cities, or struggling to get across the Mediterranean, don't care about their posture. Worrying about 'good posture' is a luxury of the industrialised world.

The six-year-old in the restaurant has perfect posture but, interestingly, we don't think about it that way. No one ever says: "Your child has perfect posture!" or "Look at that toddler's beautiful posture!" Alexander teachers like to use the word 'poise' rather than posture, but even that doesn't adequately describe the thing that children have: there isn't a word for it. It is something light, balanced, lively, lithe, buoyant, effortless, moveable, energetic, flexible, fluid, graceful.

But, sadly, the fourteen-year-old has lost it. She clearly has bad posture, but she has also lost lightness, balance, liveliness, litheness, buoyancy, effortlessness, movability, energy, flexibility, fluidity and grace. I sometimes think of it as a fall from grace, but into what? Disgrace?

It's at this point that posture becomes an issue. We start working out strategies to get ourselves into whatever shape we think is right, or go and consult bodyworkers on which bits to align, or to strengthen, or tighten, or squeeze to get ourselves upright. But it doesn't occur to us that we can get back all the other things that we had when we were six.

Adult 'good posture' is an attempt to emulate what children have, but it is very static in comparison. It gives us an approximation of the uprightness, but at the expense of even more of the flexibility, effortlessness, movability, buoyancy and balance we have lost since childhood.

What the Alexander Technique teaches, uniquely, is not good posture, but how to get back all those qualities we had as children. There's a sense of freedom and aliveness, mind AND body, and it's very different from how most adults experience themselves and life.

Mind and body? Yes. Let's have a look at some body-related stuff and then go into the mind-changing aspects.

3
The effortful life

"Is it, I would ask, likely on the face of it that the right position in which a man or woman should stand for health's sake should be one needing positive strain to preserve? The thing is preposterous."
F. M. Alcxander

Something happens to us between the ages of six and fourteen. How do we go from being effortless and natural to something so unnatural and effortful in those eight years? How does the gracefully upright child turn into the graceless, unbalanced, unattractive adult?

It is not because we become bigger and heavier. Look at this picture of my son watching television when he was eighteen months old. His head is much heavier in proportion to his size than the Phone Zombie's is, and yet it is effortlessly balanced above his body.

Sitting

Nature gave us a system for staying effortlessly upright. The network of muscles connecting the spinal processes – the knobbly bits of the spine – will hold us up if we allow it. The spine is self-erecting – it will elongate effortlessly using muscles we have no control over and can't strengthen or exercise. No matter who you are, this way of being is available to you: inside every slumped person, there's a light springy spine waiting to be liberated.

I can get most people standing, sitting and moving EFFORTLESSLY upright, within a couple of minutes, no matter how heavily curved they usually are. It can be very surprising to anyone who has been 'working at' holding themselves up so they don't slump, or who has spent a lot of time and effort developing their fictitious 'core muscles'. Some people are so relieved they cry.

There's a feeling of everything being suspended from the skull rather than stacked up from the ground like a pile of blocks. My trainee teachers and I call this effortless state 'UP!'

Look at the picture of the toddler again. He clearly isn't doing any work to hold himself upright – he's *floating* UP. And here's a picture of an Alexander teacher sitting in the same way.

It's effortless – an effortlessness that is outside most people's experience. Most people have to use muscles to get themselves into that shape. Someone once told me she didn't like seeing me sitting upright because she felt lazy not sitting like that herself. Lazy?! Sitting UP the Alexander way is EASIER than slumping!

Standing

When I was 51 and beginning to turn grey at the edges, a very polite young Japanese tourist offered to give up her seat on a train for me. I thanked her with a smile and turned it down. Why would I need a seat? Standing is effortless.

But not for most people. Standing on my commuter train, I watch people jostling each other on the platform and scurrying onto the nearest carriage, anxious to get a seat. The successful ones 'flump' into their seats while the unlucky ones stand, or lean, looking at them enviously.

When they stand or sit, most adults end up with two choices: the 'lazy' one and the 'holding myself up' one. An acquaintance of mine takes the "lazy" option to extremes. He stands, curved over at almost 90 degrees until he remembers he's not supposed to do that and so hauls himself to upright. It takes so much effort he can't sustain it for long. A medical student told me that, when she realises she is slumped, she pulls herself upright, but it only lasts about 30 seconds.

Most people think they

only have these two options, but there is a third one: the elegant, natural, effortless thing.

Smartphones didn't exist when Alexander was alive, but this drawing is based on a photo of him when he was a white-haired older man, floating elegantly upright as he's reading a business card.

Some people find the natural, effortless option difficult because they feel it can't be right. Like the idea that medicine only works if it tastes foul, they want to get down the gym and *work* at their posture and they want to do weights and exercises to sort out their back pain. They don't want 'namby-pamby' floating. For them being effortless might be, well, *effortless*, and their pain might have gone, but it's not *right* because effortless is just a variation on lazy.

But there's another problem with the 'holding myself up' option. Once we can only keep ourselves upright by *making an effort* to be upright we then need to decide HOW to be upright. Many of us then start making choices about what kind of body image we want to project. Some of the choices people make can be very funny. We'll talk about this more in the next chapter.

Many of us decide we want to be the 'right' shape, but this is fraught with difficulty. How do we know what 'right' is? The thing you think looks right, even though it takes lots of pulling to stay that way? The way your favourite celebrity stands? The thing that *feels* right, even though it isn't upright? Engaging core muscles the way your Pilates teacher taught you, or 'grounding' yourself like your yoga teacher said? Or aligning your key points, like your physio recommended? The way that feels tough and manly? Or cool? Or doesn't make your bum look big? Or shows off your bosom to its best advantage? Or hides it? Surely life should be simpler than this? And that's just being upright. As we'll soon discover, movement is even more of a minefield.

For a lot of people, the choice of upright is what I call 'beyond upright' because we have a perception that the 'sergeant-major' way of standing is, strangely, what we should aspire to. Alexander himself said disparaging things about this back in 1910. Look at this drawing of a photograph he published in one of his books. As he said, the idea is preposterous!

Many of my new clients come to me because they have back pain. They have been using all sorts of strategies to keep themselves upright. Or they have allowed themselves to slump. I'm sure you can see why both the beyond-upright sergeant-major and the slumping Phone Zombie get neck and back pain.

The 'slumper' wonders what to do about it but the sergeant-major thinks he's got it right and wonders why he's in pain. Something similar happened to me.

Moving

I can remember when I was ten, when, presumably, I was still moving effortlessly, watching one of my teachers writing on the noticeboard like this...

I wondered why he didn't just do it like I would have (*see left*). But at about seventeen I recall being horrified when I caught myself doing the same thing.

And I remember how 'effortfully' I lived until I discovered the Alexander Technique in my early thirties. Twice in my teens I had decided to change the way I walked because I wanted to appear cool. And when I was about 23, I had started pulling my shoulders back in an attempt to make them look broader. So by the time I came to the Alexander Technique I was aware of my body all the time: the pull to keep my shoulders in the 'right' place and, as a consequence, the tension in my neck. I remember the effort of getting out of a chair, or walking or running, and the not-quite-knowing where to put my hands when I felt people might be watching me.

My friends teased me about my funny walk, which seemed strange to me. Couldn't they see that this way of walking was cool?

Letting go of effort

Then I met a nurse who had broken her back trying to stop a patient falling out of bed, and she recommended I try the Alexander Technique because it had helped her learn to walk again. I went for my first lesson, like everyone else, expecting to have to do exercises or pull my shoulders back differently. Instead, I was shown how effortless everything can be – how to move, and be upright, the way I did as a child. The Alexander Technique hasn't given me better awareness of body, it's given me NO awareness of my body. It's so light and easy, I can't feel it's there.

My role model for the Alexander Technique is my cat Sigmund. His body is so light and easy, I don't think he knows it's there. He doesn't ever check it for sensations, or pull it into a shape that he thinks is 'right', or decide how to move. He just responds to his environment, and his body naturally does whatever it has to do for him to stalk a bird, run from a dog or stretch out in the sun.

If he's stung by a wasp he knows he's got a body, and, similarly, so do I when I go to the dentist. I had a bone-marrow biopsy; I was very aware of my body while that was going on. When I hold out my hand, and Sigmund rubs his head against it, purring, he probably knows he's got a body. And, of course, there are good-quality human sensations when I'm very glad I know I've got a body. But the rest of the time being aware of your body, and having to make decisions about how to use it, is a terrible burden.

Even having to make 'positive' choices about your body, like 'engaging core muscles' is a burden. It would be simpler to let go of your body and be like Sigmund, or like the six-year old. That's what Alexander teaches.

Let's have a look at some of the strategies we use to be upright and to move.

4

Our frustrating search for solutions

"Fixed ideas and conceptions are the cause of the major part of [people's] difficulties."
F. M. Alexander

We think we can learn 'good posture' and strategies for moving well from physiotherapists, or from yoga or Pilates, or by engaging those mythical 'core muscles', or by reading eight pages on how to run. Surely it should be simpler than this?

I once did a presentation on the Alexander Technique to a group of people who were studying ergonomics. When I asked for a volunteer, a physio came up to the front. It took me longer than usual to get across to her that she could sit effortlessly floating, because she already had her professional view on how to sit correctly.

She slumped, and when I gently invited her upwards she pulled herself into 'beyond upright'. When I asked her to let go, she slumped again. This happened several times – remember, these are the two choices most people think they have – but eventually she let go and sat my way.

"This is effortless!" she said, amazed. "Effortless?"

her colleague asked. "Yes, effortless."

"It can't be!" her colleague said. Be careful who you go to for advice! Strategies for staying upright and not slumping, such as 'core stability', are invented by, and for, people who have no idea how to float effortlessly like children.

They're not easy either: one of my new clients told me she had been trying to stand the way she had been taught in a Pilates class, but it was hard work and made her back pain worse. I said that if she pursued the Alexander Technique she wouldn't want to continue with Pilates as a way of being upright.

"Good," she said. "Because if anyone ever mentions core muscles to me again I'm going to slap their face!"

Surely standing straight should be simple? As Alexander said, the idea that it should take work is preposterous. Interestingly, the same woman also said about her first experience of the Alexander Technique: "This is more like Zen than about posture."

She was right!

We are not who we think we are

Adopting our own strategies for how to hold ourselves and how to move tends not to work either – it either backfires and makes us look sillier, or causes tension and pain.

A young woman came to me with back pain and it was clear to me that it was caused by her mistaken idea of what good posture is like. She stood, and sat, with her back tightly held beyond upright, a bit like the sergeant-major. Unfortunately, the room I was using didn't have a mirror so when I got her to sit floating effortlessly – and painlessly – UP, she didn't believe she looked better.

She said: "I'm not going to sit like this; this is how my mother sits. I'm slumped, I'm sagging and my breasts are on my stomach."

I bought a full-length mirror and took it in the next week.

When I showed her how my effortless, pain-free way of sitting was not how she imagined, looked better than her way, and was nothing like her mother, she wept for a long time. She had spent years working hard, and thereby causing herself pain, trying not to be something she already wasn't. As Henry David Thoreau said: "The mass of men live lives of quiet desperation."[4]

There is a phrase that AT teachers inherited from Alexander himself – Faulty Sensory Appreciation. We tend to call it FSA. Most of us, like that poor woman, FEEL we're doing something we're not. We're interpreting wrongly the feedback from our bodies. Alexander teachers have a simple way of illustrating this: we ask people to close their eyes and move their arms up to horizontal either side of them. When they open their eyes most people are surprised to find that their arms are not horizontal.

A good example of FSA was a man I used to teach whose upper back was heavily bent forward. He knew he was curved because he could see it in the mirror, but he had been that way for so many years he'd got used to it and *felt* that he was actually upright. When I got him floating up straighter, he felt he was falling over backwards to such an extent he felt unsafe and had to hold on to something. In reality he was more balanced and therefore less likely to fall over.

When my tango club moved from a church hall to a proper dance studio with a wall of mirrors, I saw a lot of dancers noticing what they looked like for the first time, and some of them were very surprised. A few realised that the thing that felt upright was stiff

---

[4] Henry David Thoreau, *Walden,* chapter 1, p. 8 (1966). Originally published in 1854.

and forced, others that they raised their shoulders and hunched themselves. Faulty Sensory Appreciation in action!

But there is another phenomenon, similar to FSA, which many people also suffer from. I call it Faulty Image Syndrome. Some of those dancers were disappointed by the way they looked because the things they were doing, and the ways they were holding themselves, weren't making them as cool or elegant as they had believed.

Just as some people who come to me for help feel they're slumped when they're not, and some feel they're upright when they're not, some people feel they're cool when they are not. Others feel the things they do with their faces and muscles make them come across as 'important' when, sadly, they don't.

This mismatch between how we come across to people and how we think we do can be very sad. A bit like the most 'uncool' thing ever, I'm sure we all agree, is someone *trying* to be cool. People I see wearing dark glasses on the London Underground would probably be disappointed to know I'm wondering how bad their visual impairment is, and whether I should offer to help them off the train. As Heidi Grant Halvorson says in *No One Understands You and What To Do About It* "Statistically speaking, there are only weak correlations between how others see us and how we believe we are seen."[5]

---

[5] Kindle edition: location 144.

Early in my Alexander teaching career I came across one of the worst examples of Faulty Image Syndrome. He was a man of about 40, slimly built but very tense and rigid. His neck, shoulders and back all hurt. When I got him to stand and move effortlessly – and painlessly – he would say: "But I feel like I haven't got any muscles."

This is a very strange thing: why would anyone want to go through the world 'feeling' their muscles?

Worse was yet to come though. One day, when I got him to free up and stand in a light, easy, elegant way he asked me: "How are my staff going to respect me like this?" He was using all that tension, causing himself pain and making himself look silly, trying to project an image of importance at work.

Here's a cautionary tale from *No One Understands You and What To Do About It*:[6]

When a friend of mine began his new position as the head of an editorial team, he deliberately sought to convey to his new employees the sense that he valued everyone's point of view. So at team meetings, he made sure to put on what he calls his

---

[6] Kindle edition: location 829.

'active listening face' while others were speaking. After a few weeks of meetings, one team member finally summoned up the courage to ask him the question that had been on everyone's mind.

"Tim," the employee asked, "are you angry with us right now?"

"No, no," he replied. "This is my active listening face."

"Oh. Well, just so you know, your active listening face looks really angry."

A classic example of Faulty Image Syndrome. Halvorson goes on to explain how to change what you do in order to give the impression you want. I think it's much simpler than that: if Tim wanted to appear to be 'actively listening' to everyone why didn't he just ACTIVELY LISTEN to everyone instead of *acting* that he was listening?

In the example above, my client was doing things to his body in an attempt to be respected by his staff. Is it really possible to DO being worthy of respect? Are his staff really going to respect him because of something he's doing with his body?

As Alexander said, the idea is preposterous. Why not just behave in a way that they will respect – treat them fairly, listen to them, make sensible decisions. Isn't that what a good manager would want to do anyway?

And what about leadership? I can't imagine explorer Ernest Shackleton, about whose leadership skills whole books have been written, having to tighten his muscles to get his men to follow him.

Making cosmetic changes to your shape or face muscles so that you come across as important MAY work. But the definition of 'cosmetic' is that it affects only the appearance and not the substance. Acting important is not going to make you important!

Trying to adopt the 'right' shape

Maybe these are extreme examples, but I suspect most of us have tried to put on the 'right' face, or adopt the 'right' shape.

But, again, what *is* the right shape? It isn't what people think of as traditional 'good posture'. You might think you look better when you pull your stomach in and your shoulders back, but I'm going to give you three reasons not to do it.

First, how far can you pull your shoulders back anyway? A centimetre? How far can you pull your stomach in? Two centimetres? Is it really worth doing all that work to make such a tiny difference? Most of my clients agree that it isn't after I've got them to try it in front of the mirror. Some of them take a long time to let themselves drop it though, because they have become attached to their faulty self-image. They feel that if they let go of muscle tension and their familiar shape they're letting go of their femininity, or masculinity, or their importance

I tell them to practice it at home. Pull your stomach in if you feel unattractive when you're at work or in the pub, but don't do it in your kitchen when you're on your own. Doing all that work when no one can see the benefit would be preposterous!

Second reason. I make a proportion of my living

from undoing the shoulder- and neck-pain, and damage, caused by people pulling their shoulders back, or trying to stand in the 'correct' way. And pulling your stomach in, clenching your buttocks – as advised by certain fitness instructors, women's magazines and spin doctors – or altering the tilt of your pelvis all restrict your breathing. You might need that oxygen!

But the main reason not to pull your shoulders back and flatten your stomach is Faulty Image Syndrome: it won't make you look the way you want it to. Try this experiment in front of a large mirror. Let yourself be lightly upright and watch yourself walk as naturally as you can. Now do whatever you need to do to pull yourself into 'good posture' – flatten your stomach, pull your shoulders back. It's a lot of work for little improvement, right?

And now watch yourself walk. You'll probably be moving in a stiff, unappealing way. Any 'cosmetic' changes you choose to make to the shape of your body will make you MOVE in a sillier way. Believe me – you look better with the extra centimetre of stomach and a natural way of walking than you do when you hold yourself in the 'right' shape and move stiffly.

If there is one natural way to move, by definition everything else is unnatural, and, sadly, as Balk and Shields say about running, can be anything from humorous to downright ghastly.

Think it doesn't apply to you? Are you sure you come across the way you think you do?

5
You don't look the way you think you do

"The uncomfortable truth is that most of us don't come across the way we intend."
Heidi Grant Halvorson, *No One Understands You and What To Do About It*[7]

Faulty Sensory Awareness and Faulty Image Syndrome mean you probably don't look the way you think you do. Some people look better than they think; others don't come across as well as they imagine.

Ever caught sight of your reflection in a shop window and been surprised by the way you look? Do you dislike seeing photographs of yourself? We lie to ourselves in mirrors and selfies. Shop windows and photographs tell us the truth.

Why do we hate seeing photographs of ourselves so much? We're so used to watching newsreaders and television presenters with their bright, neutral faces and elegant body language that we assume we look like them. We do look like them in selfies

---

[7] Kindle location 112.

because we arrange ourselves the way we want to be seen, but that lasts only as long as we can see ourselves on the screen of the phone.

The rest of the time, the reality can be a shock. One of my clients told me she had seen a photo of herself her colleague had taken and had to stop herself from crying.

So how do we actually look? You can see clues all around you – the commuter train is a good place to start. There used to be an advertisement on the London Underground for a free newspaper. It said: "You've got your Tube face on. It's like your asleep face but with your eyes open."

It's so true. Your fellow passengers are either buried in their phones, moving bits of coloured fruit around on their screens, or deep in their thoughts with their faces on 'screensaver'. I'm not being judgemental here; I'm sure that some people enjoy being able to switch off and daydream on their daily commute. I'm talking about the mismatch between how we think we look and how we do.

I saw one man on the Underground who had clearly spent a long time in front of the mirror tapering his sideboards and carefully sculpting his moustache and Frank Zappa-like tuft of beard. But his face was completely switched off, mouth drooping open, his mind 'miles away'. Maybe he didn't mind how strangers saw him, and maybe he switched his lively face on when he met his friends or walked into a meeting. But given the care he had obviously taken over his appearance, I suspect he would have been shocked by the mismatch if he had been shown a photo of himself. Faulty Image Syndrome!

There are people who wouldn't go out in an un-ironed shirt, or with no makeup, or unshaven, or with their hair uncombed, but are happy to switch off their faces on the train.

I'm sure that before they left home, combing their hair and checking themselves in the mirror, they looked awake and sparky, and assumed they were going to look like that all day. Yet once they turned away from the mirror they did their 'where are my keys?' face, or their 'oh no – is that the time?' face. On the way to the station they did their 'hurrying' face. And when they got to work and sat at their desks they did their 'thinking' or 'concentrating' face.

There is nothing your face muscles can do to help you think, or concentrate, or find your keys, or get to the station quicker. We have 'driving faces', 'listening faces', 'puzzling faces'. We frown as we look at the sandwiches in the local café, deciding which to buy. Some of you have got your 'reading face' on right now! Your face muscles won't help you drive, or listen, or solve a problem, or read this.

When I told my girlfriend I was writing a chapter about faces, she said: "No one can help the resting position of their face." She's right, of course, but I rarely see any faces in their resting position. They are either switched off, on 'screensaver', or contorted into some activity.

In about 2005, Dove cosmetics ran an advertising campaign using 'real' women instead of the usual slim models that usually appear in ads. One of the things that made them unusually appealing and attractive was their bright, cheerful, sparky faces. I suspect many of my fellow commuters, with their switched-off, frowny faces would love to look as good as the Dove women.

There are many beautiful faces made less beautiful by what their owners are doing with them, and there are also many 'ordinary' faces made beautiful by being lively, warm and humorous. It's like 'natural beauty' shining through.

What about how we move? Seeing yourself in a shop window gives good feedback. You see your reflection and realise you're, say, leaning forward and frowning. So you pull yourself up, stop frowning and carry on. Ten minutes later you see your reflection again and… WHAT?!? You're leaning forward and frowning.

What's going on here? You're doing something you don't want to do. You're doing something you don't think you're doing. You're doing something you don't FEEL you're doing. It's FSA again – you felt you were upright but your reflection showed you weren't. And, perhaps most surprisingly, you didn't have control over yourself the way you thought you did. We think if we want to be upright, we will be upright, but it doesn't work.

Some people don't think about how they walk because they assume that if their hair, clothes and shoes look good, they will look good. Some of them are right, but some, sadly, are very wrong. Some people who get themselves dressed up for an evening out would be very surprised if they could see how unattractively they move.

And some people don't think about how they walk because they think if they get their body-shape right they'll look good. Remember: any cosmetic changes you make to the shape of your body will affect how you move. Some men check their reflection in a window and adjust how they hold their shoulders, and then walk on stiffly as a consequence. Faulty Image Syndrome!

We do things with our faces we don't know we're doing. We do things with our bodies that we don't know we're doing. We also make choices about what to do with our faces and bodies that don't have the effect we want them to, making us look stressed and anxious, and a lot less bright and sexy than we think.

It all tends to make us age prematurely. I was people-watching, sitting in a department store while my daughter was trying on ball gowns, and was saddened to see so many women going into the changing room with bundles of glamorous dresses but with frowny, switched-off faces. Your face is the bit of you that people will notice and pay attention to before they look at your clothes. You'd be better off changing that!

Some people don't like the way they look and think they've found the answer. But sometimes that answer makes them look worse. Sitting in a bar with a friend, we noticed someone who had clearly had a facelift, and was putting on a permanent fake smile. She looked dreadful – it was probably not the impression she thought she was giving.

I think she believed the smile was giving her the

'star quality' thing the Dove women had. It wasn't. It was drawing attention to her but not in the way she hoped.

Surely looking good – or just coming across well – should be simpler than this?

6
A mode for everything we do

"God has given you one face and you make yourselves another."
Hamlet

Why do we do all this unnecessary, unconstructive stuff with our faces and bodies?

I spent about six months living in a flat near the Shard, Europe's tallest building, not long after it was first completed. Tourists would come to see and photograph it. Here are some tourists looking up at the top of the Shard. Do they need to do that with their faces?

41

I used to go to tea dances at my tango club. I was often intrigued by the way people who danced so elegantly were so inelegant during the rest of their lives. One day, when the club had just moved to the new venue, I saw a man looking for the lavatories. From half way across the dance floor, he noticed a sign on a door, stopped and curved forward like this to look at it. If he needed his eyes ten inches closer to the sign in order to read it why didn't he stay upright and take another step forward?

These are both examples of people going into 'looking mode'. Most people have a mode for everything they do. I went to listen to Verdi's *Requiem* sung by an amateur choir and professional soloists. The soloists stood easily, held their music low, looked at the far end of the hall and sang. The sound seemed to be coming effortlessly from deep within them.

Meanwhile, the amateur choir were pulling effortful faces and flinging their heads and bodies around. The soloists were BEING singers but the amateurs had gone into 'singing mode'.

As a compliment, I like to tell professional singers that they don't look like they are singing, or violinists that they don't look like they are playing the violin. They smile and thank me. But amateurs don't get it. They think they are less accomplished because they're not doing enough, or not doing it right, or aren't working hard enough.

Let's imagine tourists looking up at the Shard in a 'professional', effortless way. Or looking for the lavatories in the tango club. It really is possible to look at things that easily – have another look at the picture of my son watching television. And who would you rather look like – the 'professional', simply looking with their eyes, or the 'amateur' who has gone into 'looking mode'?

The Hamlet quote at the start of this chapter is actually about makeup. Strangely, it has become socially acceptable for young women to put on their makeup sitting on the train in the morning. I find their lack of self-consciousness fascinating to watch, but it's also very interesting how they go into 'make-up mode'.

They get their mirror in one hand and their mascara in the other, and then they crane their necks forward to bring their faces closer to the mirror. I suspect that when shaving on the train becomes acceptable men will do something similar.

This is a very strange thing to do. It's much simpler to bring the mirror closer to your face than the other way round – it's exactly the sort of thing your arms are meant for! There isn't a joint at the bottom of the neck, but your arms are very moveable

and flexible. No wonder people get neck pain!

I'm going to give you some more modes shortly, but let's think about why wc do these things. When I was about eight, my primary school teacher wrote a sum on the board and asked us to put our hands up if we knew the answer.

She picked someone who, even though he had his hand up, didn't know the answer. While he looked at the sum he screwed up his face, scratched his head and kept sighing and making puzzled sounds. He wasn't working out the answer – he had no idea how to do it. And the body language and vocalising wasn't going to help him work it out in any way whatsoever. It was an attempt to show the teacher that he was really *trying;* really *thinking hard* and *working at it.*

He was ACTING that he was thinking hard. When we get to that sort of age we begin to conflate *how* we communicate with *what* we want to communicate. We think that leaning forward and frowning is what looking *is*, or that scratching our heads is what thinking *is*.

I asked one of my clients: "Have you ever noticed, near London Bridge....." and before I could finish she held her breath and did this:

She was *acting* that she was wondering if she had ever noticed. Why? I hadn't even asked her the question! And it wasn't going to help her hear the question more clearly! There was no point to it whatsoever – it was something she'd learnt when she needed to show a schoolteacher she was 'listening' or 'thinking'. She was doing what she always did when asked a question. She'd gone into thinking mode.

A lot of the things we do, the modes we go into and the acting are about pleasing or placating others – showing them what we're up to and conforming to social expectations. If your boss asks you a question you need to scratch your head, or 'hmmm...', or do something to show her that you're thinking.

In reality there is nothing you can do with your face to help you think. 'Hmmm-ing' won't help you think, nor will sighing or stroking your chin or holding your breath. Thinking is chemical activity in the brain! Just as nature gave us a system for staying effortlessly upright we were also given a mechanism for thinking effortlessly.

Similarly there is nothing your muscles can do to help you listen, or concentrate, or focus. But when we were at school the teacher would ask: "Are you listening?"

"Yes."

"Well you don't *look* like you're listening!" So we'd put on a listening face – go into listening mode. Or the PE teacher would shout: "Try harder!" and we'd put on a 'trying' face and a 'trying' amount of tension in our body.

There is a laudable campaign in Ireland, started by Alexander teachers, for chairs in schools to have upright backs so that children don't lean back and then curve their necks forward. It would be equally valuable to get teachers to realise that when their pupils are frowning at their textbooks or contorting their bodies to write it isn't a sign that they are trying, or concentrating, or focusing; they are ACTING that they are trying or concentrating or focusing. Here's what Alexander had to say about concentrating back in 1923:[8]

"Note the psycho-physical manifestations of the person who believes in concentration during the act of reading, writing, thinking, or during the performance of any other of the numerous daily activities. First observe the strained expression of the eyes, an expression of anxiety and uneasiness,

---

[8] *Constructive Conscious Control of the Individual.* F.M. Alexander. Victor Gollancz Ltd 1987 p163.

denoting unduly excited fear reflexes; in some cases the eyes may be distorted, and the whole expression one that is recognized as the self-hypnotic stare. Then turn your attention to the general expression of the face, and pass on to the manifestations of the body and limbs. You will notice that there is an undue and harmful degree of tension throughout the whole organism."

He's right – most people put "undue and harmful" tension into concentrating. He also said: "I do not believe in any concentration that calls for effort".[9] Unfortunately all these modes become what's expected of us.

One of my clients used to bend her neck, poke her head forward and frown when she was listening. I suggested she simply listen, without tightening any muscles. When she came back a week later she said she had found she could listen my way, but her mother had said: "ARE YOU LISTENING TO ME?"

Before long, our various modes begin to feel right. That man at the tango club looking for the lavatories – that's what looking IS for him. He's gone into looking mode for so long it just happens whenever he wants to look. You think you don't do these things? You might be surprised – most of the time, we're just not conscious of them.

---

[9] Alexander, *Man's Supreme Inheritance*, E.P. Dutton & Company, 1918, p,103.

Have another look at the people using their phones; people in phone mode. Why are they doing all that to themselves? Most people do things because they see other people doing them that way.

Have a look at people pushing pushchairs – a good proportion of them will be leaning forward onto them, like this:

You can push a pushchair with two fingertips and your arms soft, but most people don't. When they first have to take a baby for a walk, they just copy the way they've seen everyone else do it. No one ever starts by finding out how little work

everyday things like pushing a pushchair take.

They dive in to do them with the amount of work they've seen everyone else use. Those women on the train put their makeup on like that because, well, that's how everyone puts on makeup.

There's also a sense that a degree of muscular work *has* to be put into everything we do. It's obvious, isn't it? I have to use effort to DO stuff, right? I have to get my muscles involved in thinking or I won't be able to think. And there must be a 'right' position for doing things. Your muscles won't help you think! There is no correct position for 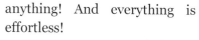 anything! And everything is effortless!

Someone at a workshop I was teaching in Canada said her back hurt when she was reading, and asked me to show her the 'correct position' to sit to read. I asked her to show me how she normally reads and she went into reading mode.

Well, I thought, no wonder she's got back pain!

Like so many people, she thought there were only two alternatives; she knew slumping wasn't good, so pulling herself upright and holding her arms horizontally must be the answer. I told her that my friend's daughter, who was then nine, said her favourite activity was reading.

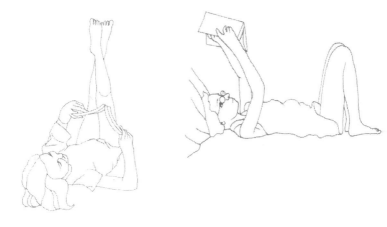

I saw her open her book at every opportunity: when she had her coat and boots on to go out and was waiting for her mother to get her little sister ready; in the two minutes before she had to leave for school; while the bath was filling.

See, there is *no* correct position for reading. You don't have to sit the same way every time you read; you don't need to go into sitting mode. Just sit effortlessly, pick up your book and open it! Actually, there are no correct positions for anything. It's like this definition of a jazz musician: "a musician who never plays the same thing once." Maybe the definition of someone who has mastered the Alexander Technique is "a person who is never in the same position once." As we're going to find out in chapter 8, if we stay free, alive and balanced we never need to be in a position.

All that trying to look good, and all the straining and/or collapsing into all those various modes comes at a cost. We make life far harder work for ourselves than it needs to be. All the scrunching of our faces and bodies ages us prematurely. And we're so busy 'trying' we miss the here-and-now and the beauty of the world around us.

As I will show you shortly, not only is everything effortless, but doing things effortlessly leads to better quality attention and better quality 'doing'.

7

Ageing is a choice

"We don't stop playing because we grow old; we grow old because we stop playing."
George Bernard Shaw, playwright, and pupil of F. M. Alexander

All those things you do with your face, like frowning to look at your PC, will give you wrinkles. You may care about that or you may not; after all, you're going to get wrinkles at some stage as you get older. And, actually, they aren't what's going to make you look old. It's possible to have a very lined face and grey hair and still look young because of your lively, smiling eyes and your light, easily-upright body.

What will age you much more than your greying hair or your ageing skin is getting your face and body stuck in a mode. I had a stall at a street festival and watched a man peering at one of my leaflets – ironically, about how the Alexander Technique can keep you youthful – like this:

The illustrator didn't have to draw wrinkles and grey hair to show that this man is older than fifty. This is what happens if you take 'looking mode' to extremes.

If you lose your effortless UP in your teens, you'll find it increasingly difficult to float upright as you get older. If, in your twenties, you curve over to check whether the screwdriver bit matches the screw like this, by the time you reach your sixties you'll be curled over your bag, holding up the bus while you look for your ticket.

You don't need to bend your back to get your eyes closer to the screwdriver. Bring the screwdriver up to your eye level!

Look at these middle-aged women consulting a map.

It would be much simpler for them to stay upright and bring the map up to where they can see it.

If, in your thirties, you have to go into 'going

down steps mode' and look at your feet to place every step correctly as you descend a flight of stairs, by the time you get to your eighties you'll do it by bending yourself at ninety degrees, concentrating on your feet. As we're about to find out in the next chapter, curving your head forward like that takes you off balance, increasing your chances of falling.

It really is possible to walk safely down stairs without watching your feet, no matter how old you are: even small children can do it.

Not only is ageing mainly caused by us getting stuck in our modes, I think ageing IS a mode. I don't believe, in most cases, our movements become restricted as we get older because we stiffen. I bclicvc we stiffen because we restrict our movements, and that we have the choice not to.

Apparently, comedian Billy Connolly wondered in one of his shows how old you have to be to make a noise when you sit down, like your father did. The answer is – you don't. You start doing it at a certain age because other people around you do it. Just as teenagers slump to fit in with their 'tribe', and the women putting on their makeup take their faces to the mirror and not the other way round – simply because that's what everyone does – you start moving differently with age because that's what you see other people do. Alexander people don't.

A colleague of mine who is in his sixties told me: "I'm younger than my peers. It's a problem."

Similarly, I don't think anyone's face will inevitably look a certain way as they get older – it's something we have a choice about.

When US president Abraham Lincoln was asked by an advisor why he had refused to accept a particular individual into his cabinet, he replied: "I don't like his face."

"But the poor man isn't responsible for his face," said his advisor. "Every man over forty is responsible for his face," responded Lincoln.

In his book *Adventures in Human Being*, Dr Gavin Francis says that, during his career as a medic, he has dissected twenty or thirty faces, many of them those of "old men with thick facial skin".[10] He said:

"There were differences between individual cadavers. Though death had relaxed their expressions, the development in their facial muscles suggested something of each individual's attitude when alive."

The muscles with the greatest variation were the ones that get the mouth to smile. "Sometimes those would be thick and well defined, implying a life full of laughter. At other times... [they] would be shrivelled to withered little strings. Sometimes I'd find a corpse whose frowning muscles had been built up to a depressing degree."

Everyone is responsible for their face as they get older. And everyone is responsible for their range of emotions – having well-developed smiling muscles sounds positive, but how can anyone let themselves get stuck in 'frowning mode'?

---

[10] Profile Books Ltd, 2015. p.44.

Can we get back our freedom of movement? Our flexible faces? Our range of emotions? Yes, we can. Research conducted by two Alexander teachers, Sarah Barker and Glenna Batson, at Winston-Salem State University and the University of South Carolina, showed improved balance and mobility in elderly people after just two weeks of Alexander lessons.[11] There's a video online showing very visible differences before and after.

The work of Harvard psychology professor Ellen Langer seems to show that ageing is just a state of mind. In studies over four decades, she showed that mental attitude can reverse the effects of ageing and improve physical health.[12]

I have helped many people learn to get back some of the lightness and ease they lost as they got older. One of my clients, aged 87, told me about something she'd noticed herself doing in her kitchen while carrying a tray. She needed to put it down ninety degrees to her right and had caught herself turning 'in one piece' by shuffling her feet round. She realised she could twist at her waist, like she used to when she was younger.

She said: "I'm never going to move like that again.

---

[11] 24 Activities, Adaptation & Aging Feasibility of Group Delivery of the Alexander Technique on Balance in the Community-Dwelling Elderly: Preliminary Findings'. Glenna Batson and Sarah Barker, *Activities, Adaptation & Ageing*.
[12] langermindfulnessinstitute.com

That's how old people move."

And faces? Yes. One of my clients used to describe her Alexander lessons as her 'Alexander facelift'. Also one of my trainee teachers, in her fifties, started looking so much brighter that one of her colleagues told her she was looking really good and asked if she had changed her face cream.

And our range of emotions? That too. One of my clients, also in his fifties, said that he had spent most of his adult life miserable, but that now he was only miserable if he chose to be.

But prevention is better than cure. Yes, the Alexander Technique can get you back a younger face and a more youthful way of moving, but if you learn it early enough, you won't need to get them back because you won't lose them. You'll never go into 'ageing mode'.

Alexander people stay looking, and acting, youthful. As my colleague said, younger than their peers.

There's a black and white film made in the 1950s of Alexander, in his eighties, looking straight at the camera, and swinging his leg around a high-backed chair as effortlessly as if he's in his twenties, a bit like this:

My colleague Elisabeth Walker, who trained as an Alexander teacher with FM himself, died a few years ago aged 99. She was interviewed on *Woman's Hour* the year before because she was still very active and teaching the Alexander Technique at 98. Someone told me he bumped into her at a conference in Switzerland when he was about to climb a mountain. She said to him she was too old to climb now, so she had taken up snorkelling. She was 91.

When I first met her, she was in her eighties but looked twenty years younger. She was upright and moved lightly and elegantly, and had a bright, lively face, full of laughter.

Here's an extract from a book about lessons with Margaret Goldie, another of Alexander's original teachers:

"I asked MG why she had a heavy, wooden-handled metal gun on her desk. She said that it would be good for use to deter an intruder – to point at him and then hit him over the head with. Whilst she was saying this to me, she demonstrated the actions. What a fearsome sight! In a flash, the energy flew to the extremities of her limbs, her whole being alive as she wielded the gun in the air. It was the *whole* of her in the action – a total action – and it reminded me of pictures I'd seen of ancient Samurai warriors in the heat of combat."[13]

---

[13] *Not To Do*, Fiona Robb. Camon Press, 1999 p.93.

She was ninety. Getting older is inevitable. Ageing isn't. You have a choice!

8
Rediscovering your 'UP', finding your balance

"The majority of physical defects have come about by the action of the [subject's] own will operating under the influence of erroneous preconceived ideas and consequent delusions."
F. M. Alexander

If you go and see an Alexander Technique teacher, you will learn how to move effortlessly, come across better and stay looking youthful. There are enormous mental benefits too – I will talk about those in the next couple of chapters.

But first let's look at how to stop doing the things that cause pain and discomfort.

Almost all our aches and pains are caused by how we go about things. Not the constant pain in your legs because you were run over by a truck. I'm talking about backs, or necks, or knees routinely hurting because we curve over screens, or stand like sergeant-majors, or the multitude of other things we do to 'misuse' ourselves.

If you're in pain because of your habits and modes you can go to bodyworkers and get 'clicked' or massaged, or you can learn to strengthen your 'core', or do weights. But as long as you keep doing things your habitual way you'll keep getting the pain. The only real solution is to change how you do things.

For instance, no amount of working on your core is going to sort out your neck pain if you keep going into laptop mode, and no amount of massage is going to stop your back pain if you keep locking your knees and curving your back to use your phone.

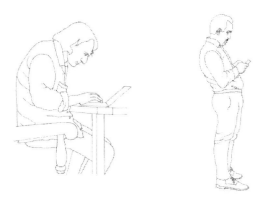

Try an experiment – get a camera and take a photograph of yourself in the mirror. If you're like the vast majority of people you did one of two things, depending on what kind of camera you've got. With a phone camera you leant back, and with a traditional camera, with a viewfinder, you curved forward and tightly closed one eye. You may not have done it as obviously as in these drawings, but you almost certainly did it – I see very few people taking photographs in a balanced, effortless way.

Looking at it logically, I'm sure you can see how crazy this is. Why distort your spine to get your camera an appropriate distance from your eyes? Why not use your arms to hold your phone further away from you, or to bring the viewfinder of your traditional camera up to your eye?

Why screw up your face to close your eye when you can just gently close it? This matters, because it's how we cause ourselves pain.

So what can you do about it? You can start paying attention to what you do. Notice when you do things habitually or go into your various modes, like taking-a-photo mode, and make new choices. Or you can get help from an Alexander teacher. Alternatively, I'll give you some ideas you can experiment with.

When we lost our effortless UP, we had to develop different strategies for being upright and for moving. These strategies tend to take us off balance and force us to bend in places not designed to bend. These three factors are the cause of most of our physical problems: losing our effortless UP, taking ourselves off balance, and bending in inappropriate places.

Effortless UP

Let's see how 'effortful' it is possible to be. Imagine that your right arm is a piece of meat hanging off your shoulder. Haul it up, against gravity, until it is horizontal, and see how much work it takes. Heavy, right?

Now let's try something different on the other side: there's a bit of air between your left arm and your flank – let that bit of air 'get bigger' and *waft* your arm up to horizontal. Easier?

You probably don't live as heavily as your right arm in that exercise, but you probably don't live as lightly as your left one either. We all know we can move that lightly and easily – we've all imitated ballet dancers or thistledown – but we don't do it.

Why would you not move effortlessly when you know you can? When we go to change a light bulb we tend to haul our shoulder, arm and hand to get our fingers to the bulb. It can be so much simpler than that: you can float your fingertips up to the light bulb, just like your left arm floated up from your side.

Try it: float your fingertips up towards the ceiling. Now pick up your phone and float it up to eye level.

It's effortless. It looks good. It doesn't give you neck pain or wrinkles. You can apply this to your life in many ways: float your hands up to your keyboard. Or float your coffee mug up to your mouth instead of curving your neck down to it. You can float your camera or your book lightly up towards eye level. It's so simple!

If you want to get an idea of the effortless UP that Alexander teaches, you can try floating your head away from your shoulders. Let your torso float up from your legs. And now let everything float up from the floor. I need to emphasis here that this isn't how the Alexander Technique is taught – it's just an exercise.

Don't worry if it doesn't feel familiar, or feels 'wrong'; by definition, anything new is bound to feel different. I'm not suggesting it should be uncomfortable or unpleasant, just unfamiliar – after all, if it feels familiar, it's the thing you already do, so nothing has changed. If it's taking less effort it's probably more constructive, and, if you do it in front of the mirror, you'll probably find that your 'key points' align – your knee, hip joint, shoulder and ear are all vertical above your ankles.

Bodyworkers like this alignment, but they usually

get you to achieve it by pulling and squeezing, not by being effortless.

Balance

When Alexander was doing the self-observational experiments that led to his life-changing discoveries, he realised he habitually tightened his neck and pulled his head 'backwards and down' during almost every activity – and that everyone else was doing the same thing. He believed this was because everyone has got stuck in the 'startle pattern'. I think he was mistaken.

The startle pattern does exist. Once, in a group class, I asked for a volunteer and a woman of about 70 came to the front. I asked her: "When did you last do a headstand?" She instantly gasped, widened her eyes, stiffened and pulled her head back.

"Thank you," I said. "You have just perfectly demonstrated the startle pattern."

We have all reacted that way on occasions, but in 24 years of teaching the Alexander Technique, I don't think I have ever met anyone *stuck* like that. Nonetheless, what we do with our heads and necks is important, because in all vertebrates, including humans, the key to switching on the reflexes that keep the spine effortlessly lengthening – vertically UP in bipeds and horizontally in quadrupeds – is the correct tone of the neck muscles.

I think people 'pull down', as Alexander called it, simply because they are out of balance. It's very easy to demonstrate how your neck muscles are affected by balance. As long as your weight is distributed equally, front to back, either side of your ankles, you'll stay light and poised, but as soon as you take your weight more one side than the other gravity tries to pull you over and you have to start tensing to stay upright.

Try it – stand easily then tip yourself back until you can feel your muscles tense. You can try tipping yourself forward, too, until you get the same effect. Both ways you will have pulled down, tightening your neck so that you don't fall over.

So, you're not going to be effortlessly UP, with all the freedom and liveliness that entails, if you're out of balance, and you will only stay balanced as long as half your weight is in front of your centre of balance and half behind – I'll draw some vertical lines shortly to illustrate this.

Ideally, when you're on your feet, standing or walking, your head will be somewhere over your ankles, and when you're sitting it will be somewhere over your hips. You'll create a lot of unnecessary work for yourself if it isn't. But, don't forget, I'm talking about being EFFORTLESSLY upright; *pulling* your head above your ankles or hips isn't Alexander!

You can have fun experimenting with all this. Don't worry if it feels 'wrong' or unfamiliar – it's new so it will feel different.

Bending in inappropriate places

I ask all my new clients to point to where they feel their hip joints are, and where they feel their head/neck joint is. They rarely point to the correct place. Most of them think their hip joints are where the arrows indicate on the left. That is the top of the pelvis. Their hip joints are much lower than that. See the arrows on the picture on the right.

And the head/neck joint – the point where the spine meets the base of the skull is not in the two places where most people think it is. Everyone seems to think the spine runs up the back of their necks!

It's here, right in the middle of the head (*on the right*).

How do so many people get to be so wrong about their bodies? We see people craning their necks to put on makeup, or to take a photo, so we start to do the same thing. We see people bend their backs and think it's normal, so we do it too.

We have even incorporated it into our everyday language. We say we 'bend down' to pick something up.

Nothing needs to bend when you pick something up. The whole idea of bending is crazy – I can think of very few activities that need the spine to be bent.

Once we start 'misusing' our bodies like that, it feels as if we have joints in places that there are no joints, and before long bending that way feels normal.

So how can you pick something up, or touch the floor without bending? Simple: you can fold, or hinge at your joints. It's what children do. It won't hurt your back, and it looks so much better!

Here are some more examples of the things we do that cause pain, and the alternatives. Strangely, most adults don't like to use their flexible arms. They would rather bend their less-flexible backs and necks.

They bring their eyes to their cameras, or makeup mirrors, rather than vice versa. We curve down to take a sip of tea, or to light a cigar.

No wonder we get back pain.

Staying effortlessly upright and floating your hands up to your face is so simple, and so elegant. Of course, this doesn't mean you have to float your phone or book horizontally in front of your eyeline.

You've discovered that new joint in the middle of your head that will allow you to

look down without having to
bend your neck.

Remember Alexander looking
at the business card? I said in
chapter 6 that "if we stay free,
alive and balanced we never
need to be in a position." He's
clearly not gone into reading-a-
card position.

Another popular way of
'misusing' ourselves, which contributes to back pain,
involves both imbalance and inappropriate bending.
I said that we stay balanced if our weight is evenly
distributed either side of our ankles.

If we put on a backpack, or carry a toddler or a
box of books, that becomes part of the weight that
needs to be balanced. When I pick up a box I sway
back from my ankles slightly to adjust my balance. It
happens naturally – I don't have to think about it –
and the combined weight of me-and-the-box gets

distributed evenly
either side of my
ankles. But most
people don't do
that; they adjust
the weight by
leaning back at the
waist – like the
picture on the
right.

No wonder we get back pain! Many women have told me their back pain started in their teens. In my experience this is often because they started leaning back at the waist to compensate for the weight of their bosom.

Pregnant women get dreadful back pain for the same

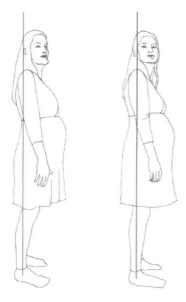

sort of reason. To hold up their bump, they lean back from their waists – where there is no joint – instead of swaying back slightly from their ankles. Look at the alternatives; when they stand the Alexander way they are floating effortlessly UP, with 'key points' much more aligned.

Men do similar things too. I used to teach a man who leant back to redistribute his weight in an attempt to look slimmer. It wasn't fooling anyone except himself; he still looked seriously overweight. When I got him to stand in a balanced way, he said he agreed that it was easier and less painful, but said he wasn't going to stand that way because he felt fat. Faulty Image Syndrome in action!

We make some strange choices about how to stand. Here's a popular one. The skeleton is unstable; without muscles we would fall on the floor in a heap of bones. The knee joints tend to fall forward so we lock them back, the hip joints fall backward so we lock them forward, and we pull our heads back so that we have half the weight of the head each side of the joint.

This locked-up way of standing is neither balanced nor effortless. There are men standing like this in my local pub every night, and when I see them I wonder if they are in pain.

Many people who come to me with knee- and hip-pain stand like this.

Some people feel they need their feet wide apart for stability but think they should have their knees together for modesty. If I stand like this it takes about 30 seconds for my knees to start hurting.

Sometimes the strategy is simply to collapse, which results in knee, hip, back and neck pain.

The best solution to all this is to learn the Alexander Technique. A good teacher will show you how to be EFFORTLESSLY upright and how to make new, more constructive, more natural choices. But I

can't emphasise enough that it is about choices and not about bodies – changing what you 'do' with your body isn't a choice that your body makes. It is a choice that you make with your conscious mind.

And you don't have to make choices *about* your

body because you ARE your body.

Consciousness; choices; change. Let's find out more.

9
Freedom to choose

"People do not decide their futures, they decide their habits and their habits decide their futures."
F. M. Alexander

It's about so much more than your body and posture...

I find it puzzling that so many people think that the Alexander Technique is about posture. Whenever I'm interviewed by journalists I tell them it isn't about posture, but they still write that it is. I had a call from a journalist asking if I could give her a few sentences about how Alexander can help back pain. I told her that I wouldn't, that she had to come and have a lesson with me so she could find out what it's really about.

She did, and experienced the freedom, effortlessness and aliveness, mind and body, that Alexander teaches. But at the end of the lesson she said: "This is not what I expected. Someone told me that the Alexander Technique would only help people with back pain if they had bad posture, and wouldn't if they had good posture."

"They obviously didn't know what they were talking about." I replied.

When the article was published, I was

disappointed to see she had written that the Alexander Technique works for back pain by improving posture.

It seems that it has always been this way. When Frank Pierce Jones wrote *Freedom to Change,* the publishers insisted that he call it *Body Awareness in Action*. Why? The Alexander Technique really is about freedom and change, and, when taught well, about having LESS awareness of your body.

I have heard anecdotally that Jones actually wanted to call his book *Freedom to Choose*. That is what the Alexander Technique is really about: freedom and choices.

One of my trainee teachers says she came to the Alexander Technique for her back pain, and – although she now is usually pain-free – the biggest benefit she has gained from it is that she now has more choices in her life. Yet she didn't try the Alexander Technique for eleven years after she had first heard of it because she had been told it was about improving posture and learning how to stand and sit properly, neither of which she felt she needed.

'Traditional' Alexander teachers get their clients to do a lot of standing and sitting. They call it 'chairwork', and it would be very easy to mistake it for learning to how to stand and sit correctly. But, as I said in the introduction, chapter titles like 'Psycho-Physical Equilibrium', 'Knowing Oneself' and 'Memory and Feeling' in FM Alexander's four books show he wasn't teaching bodywork, or how to move. There aren't chapters called 'Good Posture' or 'How to Stand and Sit in a Way that will Reduce Back Pain'.

Professor John Dewey, the influential American philosopher and educational reformer, who had Alexander lessons with FM and his brother, knew it wasn't about his body. As Jones says in *Freedom to Change*: "The greatest benefit he got from lessons, Dewey said, was the ability to stop and think before acting."[14] Dewey was talking about pausing and consciously making new decisions instead of being on autopilot.

I'm going to give you a bit of jargon. Sometimes pausing and making a new choice is simple. But frequently, during the pause, we have to keep making that new choice despite a strong urge to do things the old way. Alexander called this "inhibiting", and he came up with it before Freud started using it to mean suppressing something.

Reactions are habitual, responses are chosen. Inhibiting our habitual reaction gives us an opportunity to choose a new response.

It's about waking up and making a new choice...
Let's have a look at someone who has 'bad posture' – a professional photographer.

---

[14] *Body Awareness in Action*. Frank Pierce Jones, Shocken Books, 1976, p.97.

She's going into 'taking a photo mode', with all the physical collapse and curving that entails. It's pointless teaching her good posture, with pulling and squeezing and effort – she just needs to learn not to go into a mode when she uses her camera.

If she came to me because of her neck pain, or the realisation of how inelegant she looks, I would start by showing her how to go UP – how to switch on the reflexes that hold her effortlessly upright. Activating those reflexes involves her switching on alertness rather than making choices about her body or posture.

Then, I would show her how to float her camera to her eye rather than curving her back to get her eye to her camera. It's so simple!

The problem is that the thing she normally does, with all that scrunch and tension, FEELS right to her. The new thing, which is effortless, feels wrong. So she has to learn to do something that initially doesn't feel right. How? By stopping, inhibiting the thing that feels right, and making a new choice. By stopping and thinking before acting.

Someone I met socially told me she had taken up the harp in her fifties and was finding it very painful. I got her to play her harp and watched as she curved herself down to the instrument and the score. Classic 'poor posture'. When I gently encouraged her to float effortlessly UP and to concentrate less, she started crying. She said that when she had learned the piano as a schoolgirl, every time she got a note wrong her teacher, a nun, would whack her on the hand with a ruler.

She was concentrating so intensely, and causing herself pain, because she couldn't allow herself to get it wrong. It's pointless telling someone like this to 'sit up straight' or 'engage core muscles'. She had to learn to make a new choice – to allow herself the freedom to make mistakes.

Freedom to Change also says this about Dewey:[15] "Intellectually, Dewey said, he found it much easier, after he had studied the Technique, to hold a philosophical position calmly once he had taken it or to change it if new evidence came up warranting a change. He contrasted his own attitude with the rigidity of other academic thinkers who adopt a position early in their careers and then use their intellects to defend it indefinitely."

Stopping and thinking is about making choices; about responding rather than reacting habitually. Being able to change your opinions and beliefs is about flexibility and open-mindedness, and not getting stuck in your ways. If you are convinced you are right you are imprisoned by your opinions. To paraphrase Bertrand Russell: the problem with the

---

[15] *Body Awareness in Action*. Frank Pierce Jones, Shocken Books, 1976, p.97.

world is that fools and fanatics are so certain of themselves and wiser people so full of doubts.[16]

One of my clients once told me that, thanks to her Alexander lessons, she could now stand on a crowded train without having to hold on – it had improved her balance. But, she also said, she found it very annoying. "I used to enjoy having an argument with a colleague and sulking for an hour afterwards, but now I can't enjoy it because I've realised I can choose not to!"

Being able to choose not to argue and choose not to sulk – freedom to make a new choice!

In 2002, Victorinox, the company that makes Swiss Army Knives, introduced the Alexander Technique to the workplace. All their 900-odd employees had group Alexander classes, and one-to-one sessions were available for people who had physical problems. Within five years, absenteeism at Victorinox, from sickness *and* from accidents, had dropped by more than 40 per cent, giving them an extra 20,000 man-hours per year.[17]

I can see how changing what you do with your body might reduce the amount of sickness, but how

---

[16] He actually said: "*The fundamental cause of the trouble is that in the modern world the stupid are cocksure while the intelligent are full of doubt.*" In Bertrand Russell, *Mortals and Others*, 'The Triumph of Stupidity', May 10, 1933, p.204, Published by Taylor & Francis e-Library, 2009 (Google Books Preview).
[17] *The Congress Papers*. STAT Books. 1999.

did it reduce the number of accidents?

I'm going to give you some more jargon. Alexander said, in his Edwardian language, not "I have a goal I want to achieve" but "I have an end I want to gain".

I know this phrase was current when he wrote his first book in 1910 because the protagonist of the *Riddle of the Sands*, the first spy novel, referred to "gaining his ends". Alexander said that we tend to gain our ends at whatever cost to ourselves. Instead, we need to pay attention to the 'means whereby' we gain them. So we have these two concepts – *end-gaining* and the *means-whereby*.

When we are end-gaining, our minds and bodies are being organised by achieving a goal. The alternative is to be organised by the process (the *means-whereby*) of achieving the goal. It is important to say here that there is nothing wrong with having 'ends', with having goals, plans and dreams, but how we go about achieving them matters. For instance, having your ankles, knees, hips, shoulders and head/neck joint aligned vertically is a good 'end' if you want 'good posture', but pulling and squeezing yourself into that shape is not the best way of gaining it.

Letting yourself float upright is a better means-whereby, and will result in your points aligning effortlessly. Running while focusing on getting a personal best is end-gaining; enjoying the run is attending to the means-whereby.

When we are end-gaining we become narrowly focused and miss out on what's around us. And with what consequences! One of my trainee teachers posted this on our Facebook page:

"Saw mobile phone zombie on my way to the bus this morning: oblivious of the sunshine, blue sky, pink cherry blossom – and the pile of dog poo on the pavement. Didn't even realise he'd stepped in it, just carried on walking, eyes glued to screen. Bet he's very popular now he's arrived at the office!"

When we're end-gaining we step into the bike lane and get hit by a cyclist, or cycle into pedestrians, or trip over that box at the knife factory. Or step in dog poo.

The Alexander Technique shows us how to pause before we act – like Dewey – and make a new choice. We learn to pay attention to *how* we do things, and in the process become more aware of where we are and what's around us. It's more difficult to have an accident when you're making choices about things instead of doing them habitually, and when you're not focused on your goal.

Let's go back to 'chairwork'. If the Alexander Technique isn't about standing and sitting correctly, what is it about? Until people have an Alexander lesson, they don't think much about how they stand or sit. Then they find they have *choices* about how they stand and sit. They're surprised how effortless it can be – so effortless they can't actually feel their body – but the point is that they have to *choose* to do it the new way after many years of doing it the old way.

The choices aren't about how they do things 'with their body', they're about 'getting out of the way' and allowing their body to do things naturally. Your body knows how to stand and sit; you just have to stop interfering with it!

Switching off autopilot and waking up

In Alexander lessons, people discover they have choices about things they didn't even realise they had choices about. And once they can choose *how* to do something, they can choose *whether* to do it. But they have to be conscious – mindful – to do it. You can't make choices while you're in your head, or daydreaming, or on automatic pilot.

I heard a discussion on BBC Radio 4 about whether animals have consciousness. My personal opinion is that great apes, elephants, cetaceans, octopuses and members of the crow family are conscious, because they are interested in themselves in the mirror in a way that my cat isn't. But I was very interested to hear one of the scientists in the discussion say: "I'm not convinced all humans are conscious." The people on the Underground who have got their 'Tube faces' on aren't very conscious.

I watched an obese woman on the train eating a packet of crisps as she stared vacantly out of the window – the 'Tube face' taken to its extreme. She was barely conscious. She didn't know where she was or even that she was eating. I hope that when she gets home there's someone there that she's pleased to see, and she lights up, but I suspect not.

I suspect she puts a pizza in the oven and switches

on the TV, still with that glazed-over look. Lives of quiet desperation...

Alexander teaches people to wake up, and to start making choices in their lives. Alexander said his Technique quickens the conscious mind and helps people control their reactions.[18] Remember: reactions are habitual and responses are chosen. He's talking about developing the ability to stay conscious and *choose* instead of doing things on autopilot.

The Stoics, the Existentialists, Reich and the Alexander Technique

Having the freedom to choose is at the heart of the Alexander Technique – and some of the world's most influential philosophies.

Stoicism and choice

I'm writing this chapter at the beginning of 'Live like a Stoic Week'. Contrary to popular belief, the Stoics didn't have miserable lives and just put up with everything. They believed the secret to happiness lay in mastering themselves and putting up with anything they had no control over.

Stoic philosopher Epictetus said: "There is only one way to happiness and that is to cease worrying

---

[18] 'Conscious mind' see: *Man's Supreme Inheritance*, 3rd edition, Chaterson, 1946, p.36. 'Control their reactions' in *The Universal Constant in Living*, Mouritz, pp 87-8.

about things which are beyond the power of our wills."[19] Why do people grumble about the weather? There's nothing they can do about it. I understand why they might be unhappy that the rain ruined their picnic or spoiled a big event, but what about the daily grumbling about it being cold or grey? British weather changes every day – why not just accept that? Otherwise they're letting something they have no control over make them unhappy. Although it's not actually the bad weather that *makes* them unhappy – unhappiness is their *reaction* to bad weather, and they can choose to respond to it differently. As Hamlet said: "There is nothing either good or bad, but thinking makes it so."[20]

In his book *Thinking Fast and Slow*, Daniel Kahneman says that the 'experiencing' part of us is drowned out by the 'evaluating' part.[21] It is possible to choose to experience weather without having to evaluate it. You have other choices too: put on another layer and carry an umbrella. The Scandinavians say there is no such thing as bad weather, there is only inappropriate clothing. Or move somewhere the weather suits you better.

You really can choose, like a Stoic, to accept things you have no control over and change the

---

[19] I can't find the source of this. If Epictetus didn't say it he certainly thought it!

[20] William Shakespeare, *Hamlet,* Act II, scene 2.

[21] *Thinking Fast and Slow.* Daniel Kahneman, Penguin Books, 2011 (see chapter 35).

things you have choices about. Take getting older. The wrinkles are inevitable, so why not accept them and learn to make choices about the things you can influence? Like not moving like an older person.

Give up worrying about things you can't change and pay attention to things you can: yourself, the things you do and the ways you do them. You can 'master' yourself.

The Stoics believed that every action you take should be from choice rather than from habit, appetite or emotion. This is exactly what Alexander said in his books, and what his discoveries teach us. He, too, believed we can master ourselves. He said: "For in the mind of man lies the secret of his ability to resist, to conquer and finally to govern the circumstances of his life."[22]

It's OK to have appetites and emotions, but it's not a good idea to let them govern our decisions. If I let my appetites rule me I would drink beer and smoke Cuban cigars every night, but fortunately I can rationally choose when to drink and smoke. My GP told me that he would like to live on wine and grilled meat, but chooses not to. If I let my emotions rule me, I might have words with people on the train who have their feet on the seat opposite and their MP3 players so loud I can almost hear the words, but I rationally choose not to.

It's OK to have your habitual 'Tube face' on when you're on the Underground or to bite your nails – *if*

---

[22] *Man's Supreme Inheritance*, Chaterson,1946, p.11.

you choose to do so. But most of the semi-conscious people with their 'Tube faces' on either don't know they're doing it or think it is perfectly normal – to me, it seems like a bad habit and a waste of being alive.

Sadly I think most nail-biters would like to stop, but don't know how to. If you can't stop a habit, then it is governing you.

I keep coming back to the word 'choice'. The Alexander Technique shows us how to make choices: I can sit the way that hurts my back if I want to. I can lock my knees back and stand like all the other men in the pub if I choose to. I can curve over my phone and damage my neck. I can bite my nails, or switch off on the train. Or complain loudly about the weather. Or be self-important. Or argue with a colleague and sulk afterwards – *if I choose to do so.*

I can choose to do these things or I can choose not to – I'm not stuck in doing any of them habitually. But most people who do these things don't realise they're doing them and don't know they have a choice. When I teach people that they have the freedom to make choices, they find it liberating and it makes them happier. When we stop being a bundle of habits we start to become our authentic selves – but we can only become authentic once we start taking responsibility for ourselves.

Existentialism and taking responsibility
In the introduction to this book, I said I hoped it would get you thinking about how you do things. In *How to be an Existentialist: How to Get Real, Get a*

Grip and Stop Making Excuses, Gary Cox says he hopes it will "change the way you *behave*, the way you *act*... you can only truly change the way you think and feel about your life by *acting* differently, by acting rather than simply reacting... by always taking responsibility for yourself."[23]

That's exactly what the Alexander Technique teaches us.

Cox goes on to say: "Freedom is not freedom from responsibility, freedom is having to make choices and therefore having to take responsibility."[24] Almost all our problems are caused by how we do things, but most of us don't want to change how we do things – we don't want to take responsibility for ourselves. We want things to change, but we don't want to have to change things. I've known people with high blood pressure who didn't make the advised changes to their diet and lifestyle and simply took the tablets.

Similarly, people come to me with back pain caused by the way they sit at work, but they don't want to change that – they would rather continue to do it the familiar way. They want to get fixed up. One of my clients told me he'd got a really good osteopath and had been going to her for 16 years.

What's going on here? He gets back pain so he goes to the osteopath and gets it fixed, then is free to

[23] Gary Cox, *How to be an Existentialist*, Continuum International Publishing Group, 2011, p.5.
[24] Cox, p.45.

go back to his desk and do more of what causes the pain, so he needs the osteopath again – repeatedly, for 16 years. I taught him how to choose not to do the things that were causing the pain; how to take responsibility for himself.

You can hand responsibility for sorting out your back pain to someone else by getting 'clicked', or massaged, or you can learn to strengthen your 'core', or do weights, but as long as you keep doing the things that cause the pain you'll keep getting it. You need to learn to make new choices.

Choices and responsibility. Being late once is a mistake. Being late regularly is a choice. Similarly, not-choosing is a choice. Remember the poor woman eating crisps on the train? At some point in her past, she made a choice to switch off. Probably just a little, initially, but increasingly so over time, and now she's stuck in it. She's not conscious and she's chosen to not-choose. She's very unlikely to ever find her way out without help. She needs the Alexander Technique and a good teacher.

Reich and switching off
Why has she switched off? Because retreating from the world seems like a safe, cosy place to be, even though it's only half alive. Psychiatrist Wilhelm Reich, who worked as one of Sigmund Freud's assistants but then fell out with him, believed that we can't live full, neurosis-free lives unless we are capable of having potent orgasms.

Reich wanted people to work on their sexuality to improve other areas of their lives. To me, it's the other way round – switching off, like the lady on the train, or even just reducing your aliveness will lead to a less potent sexual response. You won't have complete orgasms if your body is too stiff, or too switched off, to move appropriately; or if your mind is still in the office or giving yourself marks out of ten. Change your consciousness and you can change your orgasms.

Anecdotally, the one benefit almost all Alexander teachers say they have got from learning the Technique is better sex.

But Reich was onto something. He said: "The sexual resignation which characterises the overwhelming majority of people means indolence, emptiness in life, paralysis of all healthy activity and initiative, or brutal, sadistic excess; but at the same time it provides a relative calm in life. It is as if death were already anticipated in the way of living."[25]

My train lady has got that relative calm in life, at the expense of losing consciousness and choices, and the freedom they bring. Switching ourselves off may save us from negative emotions and difficult experiences, but it also switches us off from positive emotions and joyful experiences.

It's so sad! It is as if death were already anticipated...

There's another way in which we cut ourselves off

---

[25] David Zane Mairowitz, *Reich For Beginners,* Writers and Readers Publishing Co-operative, 1986, p.65.

from the world. Reich called it Body Armouring; Character Armouring. We tighten our muscles to stop ourselves from feeling things. As David Mairowitz puts it in *Reich for Beginners*: "People form a kind of ARMOUR to protect themselves, not only from the blows of the outside world, but also from their own desires and instincts."[26]

And J. C. Segen's *Concise Dictionary of Modern Medicine* says:[27] "Body armour is thus a constellation of postures and expressions that mould to a personality and protect it from the world."

Switching off or tightening muscles to protect ourselves – is the world really that unsafe? As the harpist found out: no, it isn't.

Being Your Authentic Self versus Being For Others
Here's another Existentialist concept: Being For Others. Being For Others involves letting other people, in the words of Professor Thomas Flynn, "determine the 'identity' to which we try to conform".[28]

I said in Chapter 6: "A lot of the things we do, the modes we go into and the acting are about pleasing or placating others – showing them what we're up to and conforming to social expectations."

---

[26] David Mairovitz, *Reich for Beginners*, Writers and Readers Publishing Co-oerative, 1986, p.31.
[27] Segen, McGraw-Hill, 2006.
[28] *Existentialism: A Very Short Introduction*. OUP. 2006, p.73.

This is Being for Others in action.

We spend so much of our time defining ourselves by what we think other people think of us. When I was in my teens, I pulled my shoulders back and changed the way I walked, causing myself pain and tension, because I cared what people thought of me. Cox writes amusingly about how Sartre despised moustaches and saw them as the ultimate symbol of middle-class smugness.[29] Why would you choose to shave your face and leave just that bit? Because of how you want other people to perceive you.

If everyone else disappeared in a puff of smoke and you had the world to yourself, would you still shave all your face except the bit between your mouth and nose? Or, would you still shave your legs and armpits, or use makeup if no one was ever going to look at you again? What would you do with your hair? Or if you could drive any car you wanted, would you still choose a flash one with personalised plates – what the Americans call, perhaps appropriately, 'vanity plates' – if no one would ever see you?

I'm not saying you shouldn't do these things, I'm suggesting you ask yourself why you do them, and whether you really need to. Why do you care what complete strangers think about you? Your friends don't care about your hair, or your moustache or your car – if they do, you need better friends!

I said: "Defining ourselves by what we *think* other

[29] Cox, pp.74-5.

people think of us." How do we know they think what we think they do? Remember Faulty Image Syndrome? When I was having my hair cut, I heard the customer next to me tell the barber he was going to buy his first car. The barber replied: "Well, you've got to have a BMW or people will think you're no-one."

Only people who care about BMWs care if you've got a BMW. The rest of us either don't notice what kind of car you've got or wonder whether you've chosen that one because you're worried that otherwise people will think you're no-one. Only people who like brown bags covered in LV logos are impressed by bags like that. The rest of us don't even notice your bag or, maybe, think you've got more money than taste.

All that money spent on a car, or a bag, and it's not giving the impression you think. Only people who wear dark glasses on the underground think it's cool to wear dark glasses on the underground. Only people who have tattoos are impressed by your tattoo. All that pain and effort to express your individuality, when all you're doing is a variation on what all the other members of your 'tribe' are doing.

It's not individuality, it's called individualised conformity. The best way to be an individual is to *be* your authentic self. Doing things, buying things, wearing things – it's much simpler than that.

For me, the ultimate symbol of Being For Others is the selfie stick. Why are people taking pictures of themselves in front of Buckingham Palace and not a photo of Buckingham Palace? Someone knocked a cyclist off his bike in the Tour de France by stepping backwards into the road to take a selfie. Showing his friends a picture of himself with cyclists in the background was more important to him than enjoying watching the race.

Why let other people's opinions of you influence you to that extent? Why not just let yourself be your authentic self and make your own choices? It's so easy, and it makes life so much simpler!

When you're not being your authentic self, you're either acting, posturing or hiding. The train lady is hiding. Buying a BMW so that you're not a no-one – that's posturing. All those things you do with your face — it's all acting. Curving over your work and frowning gave your school teacher the impression you were working hard, but it was acting. Now it has become a habit – these days you do it for your boss. Or you *are* the boss and you *act* like you're 'actively listening', or *act* that you're important.

Acting important may fool some people but the rest will be smiling behind your back. Or you act for your own benefit; putting on that 'determined' face may make you *feel* like you're working hard but it won't help you work hard. It's an act! You don't need it! As the physicist Richard Feynman said: "The first principle is that you must not fool yourself and you are the easiest person to fool."[30]

[30] Richard Feynman, *Cargo Cult Science*: *Some remarks on science, pseudoscience, and learning how*

Acting, posturing, hiding: they are all variations on Being For Others. Trying to conform to an identity is so sad. Letting other people determine that identity is even worse. Why can't we just be who we are?

One of my trainee Alexander teachers said to me that maybe it's OK to act or posture a bit to attract a mate. But the problem is: when do you stop acting or posturing? At what point do you start to be your authentic self? The one time I met up with someone via a dating website I was disappointed, maybe naively, to find that she had lied about her age. How long do you wait before you tell someone the truth?

What hope is there for a relationship where one – or both – of the partners is not being his or herself? Talking about her divorce in *Crazy Time. Surviving Divorce and Building a New Life*, Abigail Trafford says she realised: "I didn't really know the person I was married to for twelve years."[31]

And remember Faulty Image Syndrome. How do we know that the acting or posturing gives the impression we want? Are the kind of people you want to attract likely to think you're cool for wearing your dark glasses indoors? Or only find you worthwhile or interesting because of your car or tattoo? What kind of relationship will you have if your partner was attracted to your car?

---

to not fool yourself. Caltech's 1974 commencement address.
[31] Trafford, 1993, p.8.

Professor Tom Shakespeare, the sociologist and broadcaster, has dwarfism. He said on Radio 4: "I have learned that people can still find you attractive, even if you look different. The things that make people like you, and even desire you, are mostly about personality – being emotionally warm, or good at conversation, especially being funny."

Your dark glasses or car may get you a date but they won't sustain a relationship. Warmth and humour will, so why not learn to be warm and humorous?

Sadly, a lot of people hope to make an impression by *doing* things, or wearing things, or buying things, because they don't actually know *how* to be themselves. I know, because I remember when my life was like that. My experience of learning the Alexander Technique, and teaching it for more than twenty years, is that it leads to authenticity and simply *being* oneself in the here-and-now.

And when people are their authentic selves, they are warm and humorous. I don't believe anyone was born cold and humourless. They have either 'achieved' coldness as they've got older or had it thrust upon them! After his family had Alexander Technique lessons, Nikolaas Tinbergen, joint winner of the Nobel Prize for Medicine and Physiology in 1973, said it led to "striking improvements" in their overall cheerfulness.[32]

---

[32] Nikolaas Tinbergen, 'Ethology and Stress Diseases', Nobel Lecture, December 12, 1973.

With the Alexander Technique, people learn to be at ease with themselves, and to feel good about themselves. When they learn to let mind and body be one they move well and have light, open faces. It's so eye-catching and attractive! Who needs an expensive car or handbag when they can have a bright, cheerful face like the Dove women, and have the confidence of someone who is comfortable in their own skin?

Alexander Technique: Zen for people who go to the pub

Just be your authentic self. Who are we anyway? Are we just a "constellation of postures and expressions"? A bundle of habits, strivings, fears, tensions and opinions? What's left when we drop all that?

A retired school teacher once came for a first Alexander lesson with me. Within a few minutes, she said: "This is 'Having No Head'. I've been looking for this all my life." The next week she brought me a copy of the book *On Having No Head: Zen and the Rediscovery of the Obvious* by Douglas Harding. She was right – it is *exactly* what I am teaching. Harding found that he could experience without evaluating, and that he didn't have to think. Or, more precisely, he didn't have to *do* anything to think. Remember all that stuff about going into 'thinky mode'? There is nothing muscles can do to help us think. In Alexander lessons, we first find out that we don't have to *do* anything to do things, and then that we don't have to *do* anything to think.

In the words of that old platitude: "You're a

Human Being, not a Human Doing."

All those modes are about doing. It is possible to put your makeup on without 'doing' it, without any effort. As we found out with the singers, things work better if you don't *do* them. Those people curving over to drink their tea or light a cigarette are *doing* it. The ones who are staying upright and letting their hands and eyes do it are just *being*.

I now spend most of my waking hours with no awareness of my body or my thinking processes. I'll say that again in case you missed it: no awareness of my body and no awareness of my thinking processes. I don't *do* anything to do things, and I don't *do* anything to think. Just like this description of the early Chinese concept of *wu-wei* by author and expert in Chinese thought, Edward Slingerland:[33]

"The ideal of 'effortless action', or wu-wei, *refers to the dynamic, unselfconscious state of mind of a person who is optimally active and effective. People in* wu-wei *feel as if they are doing nothing, while at the same time they might be creating a brilliant work of art, smoothly negotiating a complex social situation, or even bringing the entire world into harmonious order. For a person in* wu-wei, *proper and effective behaviour flows automatically and spontaneously from the self, without the need for*

_____

[33] https://thepsychologist.bps.org.uk/volume-28/november-2015/wu-wei-doing-less-and-wanting-mor

thought or exertion."

Wu-wei is about 'non-doing', but there's a big difference between non-doing and *not*-doing. An acquaintance, one of the most 'in his head' people that I know, scoffed at the idea of mindfulness. He said: "It's just sitting in a trance."

It is actually the opposite of that; it's about being completely alive. It's the people with 'Tube faces' who have switched off and are sitting in a trance. There are people who think that mindfulness involves closing their eyes and paying attention to their thoughts or their breath.

That is worthwhile but, in my opinion, it is traditional meditation rather than mindfulness. It may sound pedantic but there is an important difference. When I teach the Alexander Technique in France, the interpreters translate "mindfulness" as "en pleine conscience" – in full consciousness. That's a much better way of describing it.

For most of our active, waking hours we have our eyes open so practising being 'fully conscious' with closed eyes seems a bit limiting to me. If you learn to be mindful with your eyes closed, then you will have to find a way to translate it into everything you do with your eyes open. So why not learn to be mindful with open eyes?

Harding calls his approach to Zen "two-way meditation" – meditation in dialogue with the world around you rather than in your head. I call it mindfulness in 3D.

A trainee Alexander teacher said to me: "I don't

like Zen. It's nothing", as if it were about sitting cross-legged in a cave trying to clear your mind. It's the opposite of that, too. It's awareness in action. The Samurai used Zen to be highly efficient riders, swordsmen and archers. Remember Miss Goldie and the gun?

You really can create, negotiate complex situations, write a book, make a living and be a success in this state of non-doing. When she realised how little effort life needs, one of my clients told me, in tears: "But all my life, I've tried SO hard."

If you've had Alexander lessons from traditional teachers and thought they were about posture or sitting correctly you might find this connection between Alexander and Zen a little too far-fetched. But in 1969, Marjorie Barlow, Alexander's niece, described the Alexander Technique as "the secret of Zen for our time".

And listen to Harding on the benefits to be gained from Zen; from mindfulness in 3D. It's a long paragraph and I've edited out some of the more 'spiritual' bits:

"Typically, these will include an enlivening of the senses... and... a complex of inter-related psychophysical changes – including a sustained 'whole-body' alertness in place of the 'heady' intermittent sort... a reduction of stress, particularly in the region of the eyes and mouth and neck... a progressive lowering of one's centre of gravity... a striking downward shift of one's breathing, and in fact a general come-down... And, balancing this descent, a general uplift, including a sense of exaltation (as if one were perfectly straight-backed and as tall as the sky), an upsurge of creativity, rising energy and confidence, a new and childlike spontaneity and playfulness, and above all a lightness."

That's exactly what I've got from Alexander! Harding also quotes various Zen masters, going back to the 12th century:

- *Han-shan*: "I took a walk. Suddenly I stood still, filled with the realisation I had no body or mind. I felt clear and transparent."
- *Dogen*: "Mind and body dropped off!"
- *Hakuin*: "All of a sudden you find mind and body wiped out of existence."

Harding and the Zen masters he quotes are describing exactly what the Alexander Technique can give you. The benefits from the Technique, when it is taught well, are indistinguishable from those to be gained from Zen. Not the methods – not the bells and gongs, or sitting cross-legged looking at a wall; it's much simpler than that.

As British philosopher Alan Watts says in *Become Who You Are*: "I am rather leery of too much Zen – especially when it means importing all the incidental apparatus of Zen from Japan."[34]

He says: "The only way to enter into this state is precipitately – without delay or hesitation, just to do it." Not through 20 minutes of sitting still, or paying attention to your breath with your eyes closed.

Harding invites people to switch on their senses, especially their vision, and to get out of their head and leave their body alone. It's very similar to how I teach the Alexander Technique. I read a blog by a Zen master who said, when she "loses her attention", she can feel her body compress. Switch on your attention and your body will 'de-compress'. As I said earlier, it's simpler than thinking about the relationship between your head, neck and back – that will all sort itself out when you switch on.

Practitioners of Zen warn against mistaking the 'finger pointing at the moon' for the 'moon' itself. The finger is the teaching and the moon is the result of the teaching. Zen archers aren't learning how to shoot accurately; they're learning to get out of the way, be their authentic selves and allow the shooting to 'just happen'. Sadly, in the Alexander world, the 'chairwork', the release of muscle tension and the posture stuff – that's the pointing finger.

Some Alexander teachers have become world experts in the pointing finger and, yes, they help people in all sorts of ways. Some Alexander teachers publish books with pictures of the best way to sit and

---

[34] *Become Who You Are*, Shambala Publications, 2003. p.17.

stand, or the correct 'alignment' to polish your car. Maybe, *maybe*, reading them helps people change how they move, and perhaps helps them with their posture or neck pain. But this isn't the MOON. Alexander has so much more to offer.

All that posture stuff could be called 'bodyfulness', whereas what Alexander himself discovered was a *means-whereby* for mindfulness. It is 'mindfulness in action', 'mindfulness in 3D'. You can only make appropriate choices when you're in the here-and-now – when you're mindful.

The Phone Zombie stepping in the dog poo was, by contrast, an example of mindlessness in action. Alexander called it "stupidity in living" but I'm a little more sympathetic than that.

A colleague showed me a flyer for a course on mindfulness at a local New Age centre. It had a photo of a golden Buddha on the cover and pictures of candles on the inside, and I wondered why mindfulness has to be linked with Buddhism and candles. A few days later I had a stall at a local street festival. At the end, as we were packing up, one of my regular clients came over and introduced me to her husband. I shook his hand and said: "I'm trying not to breathe on you because we've just been to the beer tent."

The next time I saw her she said: "My husband is thinking of coming to you for Alexander lessons now he knows you go to the pub." He did.

So, don't let all this 'spirituality' stuff put you off: what we have here is mindfulness for people who go to the pub. Zen for people who aren't spiritual. No candles, no Buddha, no archery. No navel-gazing.

Living in the here-and-now

Let's go back to *end-gaining*. It takes three forms. First, trying to be *somewhere* that we're not. Then there's trying to be *'somewhen'* that we're not. And, finally, trying to be *someone* we're not. Acting important, demanding respect, hurrying instead of just moving fast, not noticing the scenery when you're driving, posturing to attract a mate, all are examples of end-gaining.

And here are some that two of my colleagues gave me: "Being so worried about what you look like and what he thinks that you don't enjoy the date, or be yourself."

"Being so concerned about the performance in three weeks you don't enjoy the rehearsals."

Most of the people who come to me for a first lesson are caught up in some kind of end-gaining. I show them how to be *who* they are, *where* they are and *when* they are: how to be their authentic selves, living in the here-and-now. Everything frees up. Their eyes brighten, their breathing opens up and they start feeling lighter and clearer. Movement and thinking become effortless.

We create such difficulties for ourselves! We put work into movement because we think movement takes work. We think we have to use effort to think, or to make a decision. We believe we have to use our facial muscles to listen, or understand, or catch a ball. We frown when we're reading Sartre because it's 'difficult'. Some of you are frowning as you read this, even though it is so simple! Everything really can be done effortlessly – so effortlessly it feels like you haven't got a mind or body. Mind and body are one. You feel clear and transparent.

I have a couple of disagreements with the Existentialists. Sartre said that we can never be in the present moment, because our consciousness is constantly rushing from the past to the future. I suspect all the coffee he drank in those cafes made him feel that way. He had obviously never had the rich enjoyment of the here-and-now that Alexander has given me.

And when Heidegger said that we can never be our authentic selves because we are constantly self-aware, he had never had the Zen experience of mind and body dropping away.

Nonetheless, the Alexander Technique has enormous parallels with Existentialism. It's the secret of Zen for our time. It's identical to what the Stoics were looking for. It's a simple, accessible way to allow *wu-wei* – effortless doing. It's the answer to the mind/body paradox.

How can it be all this? Because it's about being your authentic self, living in the here-and-now.

The Alexander Technique and your search for happiness

It is also the answer to your search for happiness. How? There are a number of reasons.

In Chapter 2, I said that small children have "lightness, balance, liveliness, litheness, buoyancy, effortlessness, movability, energy, flexibility, fluidity and grace" that we tend not to have as adults. Children also know how to be happy, but part of our "fall from grace" is that we are increasingly prepared to accept boredom and unhappiness.

Harding says the benefits of mindfulness in 3D include "an upsurge of creativity, rising energy and confidence, a new and childlike spontaneity and playfulness." It also gives us back something else we knew as children: how to seek out things that make us happy.

Happiness doesn't lie in working every day at a job you don't enjoy just so that you can make enough money to pay your mortgage, do a bungee jump every now and then, have a better car than your neighbours and go on a couple of expensive holidays every year. It doesn't lie in working hard to save enough money that you might have happiness later.

The future is a fantasy. You really can choose things that make you happy now. You have the freedom to choose to stop doing that job that you hate, to end that relationship that is dragging you down, to spend time doing things you love. Everyone is responsible for their own happiness. Alexander gives us a means-whereby to achieve it.

When you are free to make choices, it is easy to choose to do things that make you happy and to be with people who you want to be with. You can choose to stop doing things to satisfy other people's agendas and stop judging yourself by other people's standards.

I met a man who was only in his thirties and was already a consultant nephrologist. I was so impressed! But he was miserable because someone from his year at medical school was already a professor. Being For Others in action!

The contents of your head won't make you happy – they're a fantasy too. I asked one of my clients why he was being 'thinky'. He replied: "I keep trying to work out how to get back the happiness I had a few years ago." I asked him to tell me how happy he was on a scale of one to ten, and he said "four". But when he stayed mindful, he said "six". When you get out of your head you notice the blue sky and the cherry blossom, and the sunset and the birdsong. And you don't step in the dog poo.

And finally, ever heard that saying: "Happiness is wanting what you've got"? When you live in the moment you've got what you want. If you don't believe me, come and have an Alexander Technique lesson with me. I'm the happiest man I know, and one of my good friends, another Alexander teacher, describes herself as the happiest person in the universe!

10
Embracing change

*"Teachers open the door but you have to
enter by yourself."*
Zen proverb

What Alexander discovered is the secret of Zen for
our time. It teaches us how to be our authentic
selves, living in the here-and-now. It's the answer to
all our problems. But it isn't a quick-fix cure. It's a
slow and steady way of bringing about real and
lasting change.

In the previous chapter, I kept talking about
choosing and choices. Throughout the book I've
repeatedly used the words 'simple' and 'simpler'.
When you live the Alexander way, everything is
simple, from being upright to being happy. It's a
much easier way of life. But it's not necessarily easy
to achieve, because it involves *change.*

The Alexander Technique isn't humanity's next
evolutionary step, but it really could make an
enormous difference if more people applied its
principles. The world doesn't need better posture –
as I said, poor posture is a very First World problem.
The world needs more people who can inhibit, can
pause and reconsider before acting. People who are
free to change their minds and are less attached to

their opinions. People who can respond rather than react; who are in charge of their own happiness and can "govern the circumstances" of their own lives.

The Alexander Technique liberates us and allows us to change. Very occasionally there are really big changes early on. I know someone who went down to the Thames at the end of their first Alexander lesson and threw in their wedding ring. I taught a workshop for beginners somewhere in Europe and the next day one of them phoned me with some feedback. She said her father had died eight years before, and at the end of my workshop she had gone home, gone to her father's wardrobe, taken out all his clothes and delivered them to the charity shop.

These are exceptions though. For most people, the changes are slower. Dewey said, in his preface to the 1939 edition of Alexander's book, *Use of the Self*: "There were no speedy and seemingly miraculous changes."[35]

Why change can be difficult

Most people would like to change, but find it difficult. A friend told me her New Year's resolution was "to lose weight – same as last year and the year before". What hope for change is there if we can't even fulfil our New Year's resolutions? By the way, I have met very few obese Alexander teachers.

What is the difficulty with changing how we do things? Change is so simple: after tying my shoe

---

[35] Alexander, *Use of the Self*, Orion Books, 2004. p.10.

laces in a particular way for 50 years, I saw a TED talk about how to tie them in a different, better way. It took me ten days to learn to do it the new way as automatically as I used to do it the old way. Surely, it should only take ten days to learn to use your phone differently, or to stop frowning at your PC, or to stand in a softer way so your back doesn't hurt, or to stop locking your legs back and damaging your knees.

One of the reasons change usually takes longer is that we can't stop doing things we don't know we are doing. Whenever my clients lick their fingers to turn over pages in their diaries I give them some 'homework'. I ask them to notice every time they lick their fingers until I see them the following week. Every single one of them says: "I lick my fingers?!" How can we stop doing something – like curving over our phones – if we don't know we're doing it?

If we want to change, we need to stop being on autopilot and become conscious of what we're doing. That's why the homework I set my finger-licking clients was *notice* when you lick your fingers, not *don't* lick your fingers. Habits are unconscious, and the first step to changing them is to become aware of them. People who bite their nails know they do it. The reason they can't stop is that they aren't aware they're doing it *while* they're doing it. They only do it when they are 'thinky' – when they are unconscious. We can only choose to stop our habits, or do things differently, when we are conscious.

Some people don't want to change. Why would a Phone Zombie change the way he does things if it doesn't cause him pain and he doesn't care how silly he looks? I worked somewhere where the new receptionist licked her fingers before handling any piece of paper.

I pointed it out – "I lick my fingers?!" – and gave her one of those desktop sponges. She used it for a week or so, then went back to licking her fingers. Why? Not because she actually preferred licking her fingers. She found it easier to stay on autopilot than to make new choices.

Some people have other reasons to resist change. One of my first clients was a dentist with back pain. I showed him how to be effortless and he said he was pain-free for the first time in years. But he didn't come back because he said he was "too old to change". For him being in pain was preferable to learning to do things differently.

Another reason why change is difficult is that some people don't want to be conscious, they don't want to take responsibility for themselves. They want to just get fixed up. The man with the "very good osteopath" he had been going to for sixteen years had been getting his pain 'fixed' and returning to his desk and getting the pain back. Surely he could have stopped doing what was causing the problem by now if he'd really wanted to?

Someone I used to teach was permanently leaning back to redistribute the weight of her belly and bosom and, as a consequence, had lower back pain. When I showed her the balanced way to stand the pain went and, she said, movement was effortless. But she went to see a bodyworker who told her the pain was caused by one leg being shorter than the other, so she decided to get that fixed up. Why? Because it's easier to ascribe our problems to something outside our control than to take responsibility for them.

If she took responsibility and stopped doing the thing that was causing her pain she'd be more aware she could take responsibility for changing other things too, which might involve some tough choices. I got the impression that if she became conscious she would realise she hated her job, and she would have to change that. And that she'd recognise that she didn't like her husband either, and would have to change how they related to each other.

And there's yet another problem with changing what we do. The thing we already do feels right and the new thing feels unfamiliar, or 'wrong'. It's much easier to do the old, familiar thing than to choose to do something that feels wrong. As Alexander said: "This experience of passing from a 'known' to an 'unknown' manner of use of the self is the basic need in making a fundamental change in the control of man's reaction..."[36]

If the slouching medical student is to sit effortlessly upright, she is going to have to stop doing the familiar thing and learn to do something that feels new and wrong. When you did that experiment with taking a photograph, I'm guessing your usual

---

[36] Alexander, *The Universal Constant in Living*, Mouritz, 2000. p.157.

way felt right and the new way felt unfamiliar. It's why exercises won't help your neck or back pain: if your neck pain is caused by how you do things, you'll do your exercises the same way you do everything, and probably exacerbate the problem.

Accepting the unknown

Change can only happen if we learn to accept the unknown. Unfortunately, although the Alexander Technique is unlike anything they have ever done, people try to make sense of it in terms they already know.

Someone said: "It'll work better if I close my eyes and do my Yogic breathing." No it won't. And another: "But I have to use core muscles. It's taken me years to get it right. You're arguing with modern science." There are no core muscles!

Neither of them came back for a second lesson. A physiotherapist said to me: "That can't be right. You must have pressed an acupressure point." And another bodyworker said: "Yes, it's effortless. But it's not *right*. You have to lean back so your weight is on your heels, lift your chest and pull your neck back. That's *right*." It's preposterous! To paraphrase Bertrand Russell, she was either a fool or a fanatic.

The most difficult people to teach are usually self-confident men who think they already know the answers to everything, or can't allow me to know more about something than they do in case they put themselves below me in the pecking order. You're not going to change unless you let go of doing what you already believe to be right.

If what you already do works, you're not going to come to me for Alexander lessons, and if you have come to me then what you already do isn't working!

What *really* needs to change
I think many people would like to change. The evidence for this is the huge 'self-help' sections in most high-street bookshops. The problem with self-help books is that they tell us what to *do* in order to change – like live in the moment, or eat less chocolate – but don't tell us *how* to do those things.

It is the *how* that we need to know and the *how* we need to change. Alexander wrote a whole chapter on golfers endlessly being told to keep their eyes on the ball and not being able to. Being told to keep your eyes on the ball is a good 'end', but just being told to do it doesn't tell you *how* to achieve it. As I've already mentioned, we don't have control over ourselves the way we think we do.

There's a management book, written by Michael Gelb and Tony Buzan, called *Lessons from the Art of Juggling*.[37] This is its premise: take these three balls and teach yourself to juggle, but observe how you go about it, because it will be how you go about everything.

I divide the world into three kinds of people: *thinkers*, *do-ers* and *procrastinators*. Teaching

---

[37] *Lessons from the Art of Juggling: How to Achieve Your Full Potential in Business, Learning, and Life.* Michael Gelb and Tony Buzan, Harmony Books, 1994.

themselves to juggle, thinkers say to themselves: "Hmmmm. I think I'll read the manual again and watch some online videos." Do-ers say: "Right! I'm going to work on this for three hours every day and get it done by Friday!" And procrastinators say: "I'll start tomorrow."

So, you read *The Power of Now* and set about learning to live in the here-and-now. If you're a thinker, you'll try to think yourself into the present moment. If you're a do-er, you will try to work your way into it. If you're a procrastinator, you'll switch on the television. It's the thinking, doing or procrastinating – all of which are habits, and so 'known', deep-seated and familiar you don't even notice them – that are stopping you from achieving what you want to achieve; those are the things that need to change. A good Alexander teacher will invite you into a zone where you are neither thinking, doing or procrastinating – an alive, fully conscious state in which new choices can be made.

My girlfriend and I overheard a couple in a café discussing mindfulness and living in the here-and-now *theoretically*. They were clearly not practising what they were preaching and, it seemed, thinking that they wcrc. It's why I haven't addressed how to 'do' the Alexander Technique – you'll just try to do it the way you do everything.

You can't learn these things from books, partly because it is the *way* we learn that needs to change. Dewey, 'the father of Progressive education', knew this. He went so far as to say: "It [the Alexander Technique] bears the same relation to education that education itself bears to all other human activities."[38]

I have read books about authenticity and living in the moment that describe *exactly* what I am teaching: *The Wisdom of Insecurity* by Alan Watts; the *Inner Game of Tennis* by W Timothy Gallwey; and *On Having No Head*, which I've already mentioned.[39] The problem is that none of them tell you how to put their ideas into practice. And the injunction by the Vietnamese Buddhist monk Thich Nhat Hanh, to "walk as if you are kissing the Earth with your feet" sounds lovely, but how do you begin to go about it?[40] Walking like that is a great 'end' but how do you go about 'gaining' it?

If your goal is living in the here-and-now, how do you achieve it?

Alexander Technique gives us a 'means-whereby' we can achieve what all the self-help books are offering. A means-whereby to real, lasting change. The Dalai Lama says that the purpose of life is to be happy. What we have here is a means-whereby to achieve it.

---

[38] Use of the Self. FM Alexander. Orion Books Ltd 2004. P12

[39] Watts, *The Wisdom of Insecurity: A Message for an Age of Anxiety*, 1971. Gallwey, *The Inner Game of Tennis*, 1974. Harding, *On Having No Head: Zen and the Re-discovery of the Obvious*, 1961.

[40] Thich Nhat Hanh, *Peace Is Every Step: The Path of Mindfulness in Everyday Life*.

Slow and conscious: the process of change

Interestingly, when I started training Alexander teachers, some of them split up with their partners and others had changed their jobs within the first year. The changes the Alexander Technique helps to bring about are more obvious on the training courses because the work is more intense and the change happens quicker. Trainees realise they don't have to be the complicated person they were before, and their partners sometimes don't like the change. Or they find they start to be happier and their partners stay how they were. But listen to this account from one of my trainees about what can happen when both partners are learning the Alexander Technique:

"My husband and I have both been having AT lessons with Peter for some time and the following is a story about how it helped us avoid a common household crisis. One evening, when I got home, my husband told me he had lost the house keys; he'd searched everywhere, retraced his steps, but they were gone. We looked at each other. In that moment I could sense my habitual response rising: recriminations, fears about security, annoyance as we were due out to a friend's for supper... I inhibited. In the same moment, he felt his habitual response: anger at himself for losing something, guilt for not being perfect, annoyance with me for judging him... he inhibited. "Oh well," I said, "better call a locksmith."

"Yes, I'll do that."

He did, the locksmith came and we were only 15

minutes late for dinner (some of that time having been spent kissing as we were so pleased with each other - and ourselves)..."

By the way, their posture improved too!

With one-to-one Alexander lessons, change starts slowly. One approach I use is to play catch with my clients. When we start they want to get it *right!* They are full of fear about dropping the ball. They lean forward and frown to throw it to me. So I gently introduce the idea that they can do it with less effort. Most of them soon find that they can throw and catch the ball effortlessly – and very accurately – while keeping eye contact with me, and giving the ball very little of their awareness.

I point out that, if they can do that with a ball after years of being told to "keep their eye on it", they can check messages on their phones that simply. And then they can choose to be effortless every time they use their phone *and* every time they fill the kettle. And then every time they open a door as well. And so on. Slowly, consciously, mindfully, they can change how they do everything.

But there's one instruction from me that, at first, no-one can follow. I tell them that if they drop the ball, I'd like them to ignore it, and they nod in agreement. But as soon as they drop it, without hesitation they jump into embarrassed action, frowning and apologising for their stupidity as they go to pick it up. All that shame and guilt for the least important mistake they'll ever make!

I used to teach a sporty man who got cross with

himself every time he dropped the ball. One day I told him I didn't understand why anyone would buy themselves a fast car and he got cross about that too. "Some people are into cars...." he told me.

I said: "If you can't let go of having an emotional reaction when you drop a ball in an Alexander lesson how are you ever going to stop having an emotional reaction when someone simply has a different opinion from yours?"

Slowly, gently, two things happen. When people stop tensing themselves up because they care about dropping the ball, they drop it less often. And when they do drop it, it isn't a problem for them. Then they find that they can apply this to 'more important' things out in the real world, becoming less reactive and doing things more easily and comfortably. They become lighter and happier. They make fewer mistakes – because they're starting to do things consciously – and give themselves less of a hard time when they do.

They can start to choose not to do the things that stress them out, or cause them pain. And when they do things the old way they can recover their Alexander 'poise' very quickly afterwards.

Start by making conscious choices about how you relate to your phone and then maybe think about changing how you relate to your boss. Learn to make a new choice when you drop a ball and then apply it to how you deal with a colleague. Make conscious choices about tying your shoelaces and then make new choices about how you sit. Or whether to have that second slice of chocolate cake. Or if you need to scurry onto the train to get a seat before anyone else. Or whether to stay sitting in front of the television rather than go and play your piano, or read, or go for a walk. Slowly, consciously making new choices. I've just seen an advert for a *Guardian* masterclass entitled 'Reach your potential: how to switch off autopilot and make positive and meaningful changes to your life'. Positive and meaningful change is so simple! Just stay conscious and make choices!

After their first few lessons, my clients report that they feel lighter, taller, more relaxed, and – as most people come to me with back or neck problems – that their pain is reduced. These physical benefits are easy to interpret as changes in posture. Some people stop at this point, when they've got their Alexander 'yellow belt', because they've got the thing they came for – less pain or better posture.

And some people never get beyond this point because they don't notice the 'Zen' aspect to it. They might keep coming, but only to get their bodies freed-up. They want it to be more like a treatment than to have to engage in a learning process. But most people by this point have had a glimpse of the possibilities of change and freedom that lie ahead of them and keep coming back for more.

The next phase is that they find they can choose not to lock their knees back when they stop moving. Or choose to 'not-do' something – like not lean on the buggy or shopping trolley while they push it, despite it feeling wrong. Or stay conscious throughout a boring meeting so they don't bite their nails. Or catch themselves *about to* frown and curve over their phone – and choose not to. Or choose not to argue with a colleague and sulk afterwards.

Next they find that they're no longer locking their knees back, without even thinking about it. They float upright at their desk without having to choose to – and it no longer feels wrong. They become less goal-driven and less attached to their opinions. They feel happier and more comfortable in their own skin.

Then people start commenting. "Why have you stopped grumbling about your back pain?" "You've started speaking up in team meetings." "Wow, you look taller!"

One of my clients told me his wife had *stopped* commenting: "She no longer pokes me in the back with her umbrella, saying 'stand up straight!'"

Over time, they find they either drop their habits or can choose not to indulge them. Long-standing, deep-seated habits, like always hurrying, or regularly being late. Being nervous or apologising all the time. Habits of friendships and relationships.

The Dalai Lama says we remake our karma every day. Alexander students gradually find that they can choose not to let their unhappy childhood affect them. They begin to feel good about themselves, whatever body shape they inherited. They drop the things they felt were 'part of their DNA'. "I can't dance." "I need to act like I'm important." "I couldn't possibly do a talk to the whole team." "I'm not a leader."

Someone I used to teach said "I thought I was born grumpy" as he became happier.

I heard a couple of recovering alcoholics being

interviewed on the radio. The interviewer asked them about willpower and they both said kicking addiction doesn't take willpower, it takes being honest with yourself. A lot of change involves being honest with ourselves, but we find reasons to let ourselves off the hook, and so many of our choices are based on fear or fear of change. "I won't leave this soul-destroying job because, actually, it's not too bad." "I'm not happy living with this boring person, but I'll stay because it could be worse."

Thích Nhat Hanh said: "People have a hard time letting go of suffering. Out of a fear of the unknown, they prefer suffering that is familiar."

Remember that quotation from Thoreau: "The mass of men lead lives of quiet desperation?" He went on to say: "What is called resignation is confirmed desperation." Someone I know who wasn't happy was advised by a friend: "Lower your expectations. Marriage is crap. Work is crap."

That is so sad! If we realised how achievable happiness is, we would make different decisions. As clinical psychologist Pamela Stephenson says, we define happiness as absence of pain: we can do better than that.

I had my first Alexander lesson in 1988 and qualified as a teacher in 1993. For me, the benefits of Alexander keep unfolding. In my late fifties, I find myself increasingly full of humour, creativity and confidence. I'm "younger than my peers". I use my time well and my life is full of riches – not wealth, but things I love to do, laughter, people I love to be with.

I wake up every morning feeling happy with my life. My body is so effortless, I can't feel it, and I have no awareness of my thinking processes. Like the Zen masters, I feel clear and transparent. Mind and body have dropped away.

Choosing an Alexander Technique teacher

If you are going to get someone to help you change your life, you need to choose them carefully. I'd like to say all Alexander teachers are good but, sadly, it's not true.

Anyone can call themselves an Alexander teacher, even if they have had no training. And not all training courses are good. Weirdly, you can buy an Alexander Technique teacher training *correspondence course* online – make sure your teacher went to a real, live, in-the-flesh school!

The benefits of the Alexander Technique to your body and posture are 'yellow belt' but some Alexander teachers never get beyond this point. They don't get to the other life-changing benefits the Alexander Technique gives us. Alexander thought his technique could be humanity's next evolutionary step, and yet when I posted something on my blog saying "It's not about posture". I had emails from angry Alexander teachers telling me I couldn't say that.

There are many things that can be taught theoretically, but the Alexander Technique is not one of them. Unlike anything else I know, to teach Alexander you have to live it. I see martial-art instructors who are alert and lively when they are in the *dojo* but switch off again when the class finishes. I have met counsellors who have gone into the business of sorting out other people's lives instead of sorting out their own. I even knew someone who was on Prozac while she trained as a psychotherapist.

To teach the Alexander Technique, you have to have *embodied* it, to have *incorporated* it into your life. Aren't those interesting words! Trainees have to learn to teach it 'hands-on', over three years. It can't be 'embodied' by listening to lectures, or spending years studying anatomy or Alexander's books. As Alexander said: "A man should never teach others unless he has lived and experienced what he teaches."

There will be Alexander teachers out there who will be surprised by the scope of the Technique if they read this book. Some of them really do think it's a sophisticated way of changing posture or releasing muscle tension. As I write this, one of the professional bodies for Alexander teachers in the USA describes the Alexander Technique like this on its website:

A proven approach to self care, the Alexander Technique teaches how to unlearn habitual patterns that cause unnecessary tension in everything we do... By teaching how to change faulty postural habits, it enables improved mobility, posture, performance and alertness along with relief of chronic stiffness, tension and stress.

And one of the most popular and well-regarded websites dedicated to the Alexander Technique says:

The Alexander Technique is a way to feel better, and move in a more relaxed and comfortable way... the way nature intended.

If they really believe that, they've got an incomplete impression of what Alexander is about: there is a lot about bodies, posture and movement, but woefully little about thinking, or consciousness and choices. The benefits of Alexander are so much bigger than changing faulty postural habits or learning to move in a more relaxed and comfortable way! Remember the finger and the moon?

Try out a few of your local teachers and go to whichever one you feel comfortable with, and whichever one gets their Alexander message across to you in a way you can apply to your life.

Some Alexander teachers will teach you how to stand and sit correctly, or how to move without tightening your neck, or will get you aligned, or release your muscle tension, and maybe that's all you want. But some teachers will show you how to get back the lightness, balance, liveliness, litheness, buoyancy, effortlessness, moveability, energy, flexibility, fluidity and grace you had when you were six.

They will invite you into the here-and-now and teach you how to stay conscious and make new choices – it's what my **Mindfulness in 3D** teachers do.

And, finally, see if you can find a teacher who seems happy – because the Alexander Technique is the secret to happiness.

Appendix
F. M. Alexander

Frederick Matthias Alexander was born in Tasmania in 1869. As a young man he trained as an actor and started delivering Shakespearean monologues. He was building up a reputation for himself, but his career was threatened by a voice problem: during his performances he would become increasingly hoarse until he was almost inaudible.

Medics told him he was overusing his voice, so he tried not talking before his performances, and even barely talked for two weeks before an important engagement, but he still lost his voice when he was on stage. It became clear that it wasn't caused by overuse, it was something he was doing when performing.

After a lot of self-observation he discovered that the way he tightened his neck and took an audible in-breath when he was about to recite was "depressing his larynx", and that this was the cause of his vocal problems.

Stopping doing it was not easy. He had to learn to not-do the thing that felt right and start doing something unfamiliar. He gradually developed a way of consciously choosing how he went about reciting rather than relying on the habitual way, and then became free from the throat and vocal problems. It made such a difference to his voice, and to the way he moved, other actors came to him for advice: he gave up acting and started making a living from teaching his method.

He moved to London in 1904 and eventually divided his time between the UK and the USA. He died in London in 1955.

Find out more

If you would like to read more about Alexander and the history and background to his work:

Freedom to Change, Frank Pierce Jones, Mouritz, 1997.

I also recommend these non-Alexander books:

Ten Thoughts about Time, Bodil Jönsson, Robinson, 2005.
The Wisdom of Insecurity, Alan Watts, 4th edn, Rider, 1987.
Zen and the Art of Consciousness, Susan Blackmore, Oneworld, 2011.
The Inner Game of Tennis: The ultimate guide to the mental side of peak performance, W. Timothy Gallwey, Pan Macmillan, 2014.
How to Be an Existentialist: Or How to Get Real, Get a Grip and Stop Making Excuses, Gary Cox, Continuum International Publishing Group, 2011.

You can find lists of teachers at

alexandertechniqueinternational.com
alexandertechnique.co.uk

Other how-to books from the Real Press

How to become a freelance writer (David Boyle)

Techno Tantrums: Ten strategies for coping with your child's time online (David Boyle and Judith Hodge)

Fourth to First: How to win a local election in less than six months (Freya Aquarone and Steffan Aquarone)

www.therealpress.co.uk
FREE ebook if you sign up to our mailing list!

—

77707133R00083

Made in the USA
Middletown, DE
24 June 2018